Gifted or Able?

Open University Press
Children With Special Needs Series

Editors
PHILLIP WILLIAMS
Emeritus Professor of Education
University College of North Wales, Bangor.
PETER YOUNG
Formerly Tutor in the education of children with
learning difficulties, Cambridge Institute of Education;
educational writer, researcher and consultant.

This is a series of short and authoritative introductions for parents, teachers, professionals and anyone concerned with children and young people with special needs. The series will cover the range of physical, sensory, mental, emotional and behavioural difficulties, and the changing needs from infancy to adult life in the family, at school, in further education and in society. The authors have been selected for their wide experience and close professional involvement in their particular fields. All have written penetrating and practical books readily accessible to non-specialists.

TITLES IN THE SERIES

Gifted or Able?

Realizing Children's Potential

Peter Young and Colin Tyre

Open University Press
Buckingham • Philadelphia

Open University Press
Celtic Court
22 Ballmoor
Buckingham
MK18 1XW

and
1900 Frost Road, Suite 101
Bristol, PA 19007, USA

First Published 1992

*A catalogue record of this book is available
from the British Library*

Library of Congress Cataloging-in-Publication Data
Young, Peter, 1920–
    Gifted or able?: realizing children's potential/Peter Young,
Colin Tyre.
        p.   cm. — (Children with special needs series)
    Includes bibliographical references and index.
    ISBN 0-335-09997-1. — ISBN 0-335-09996-3 (pbk.)
    1. Gifted children—Education—Great Britain.   2. Special
education—Great Britain.   I. Tyre, Colin.   II. Title.
III. Series.
LC3997.G7Y68   1992
371.95'0941—dc20   92-8262
                                                                        CIP

Typeset by Colset (Pte) Ltd, Singapore and London
Printed in Great Britain by Biddles Ltd, Guildford and Kings Lynn

How much people in general are deceived in their ideas of great authors. Every sentence is by them thought the outpourings of a mind overflowing with the sublime and beautiful. Alas, did they but know the trouble it often costs me to bring some exquisite passage neatly to a close, to avoid the too frequent repetition of the same word, to polish and round the period and to do many other things. They would soon lower the high standard at which our reputation is fixed. But still the true poet and proser have many moments of unalloyed delight while preparing their lucubrations for the press and public.

Charlotte Brontë, aged 13 years

Contents

Series Editor's Introduction

'L'education peut tout.' Belief in Helvetius's aphorism fluctuates with national fortune. Today, in an increasingly competitive world, and with a demographic time-bomb ticking away – a growing ageing population accompanied by a shrinking workforce – it is to education that politicians turn once more for help. We need young people with keener motivation, better training and higher attainments. They will have to possess more advanced skills and to offer more ingenious answers to our needs. So our politicians have initiated a plethora of reforms, usually well-intentioned, though sometimes misguided, aimed at developing high-quality education for all.

In this current educational whirlpool of changing ideas and policies, the value of nurturing the gifted, Ashby's 'thin clear stream of excellence', has often been advocated. Talent is precious, it is said, and in these challenging times it is particularly important that it is identified and developed. This book certainly agrees that talent is precious; but it also argues that it is not rare. It argues that views of giftedness, based on measures of intelligence and problem-solving ability, are far too narrow, and that we must extend our idea of giftedness to include outstanding performance in such areas as physical skills, technical abilities, the arts, leadership and concern for others. These are examples of the qualities that society needs just as urgently as intellectual genius or excellent performance in a core curriculum. And they are to be found throughout the population.

In adopting this stance, the book leads on to consider how education can help develop such a rich array of human talent. With the advantage of a wealth of fascinating data, culled from research findings, as well as from the biographies of eminent people in many different fields, it stresses the importance of early education and the key educational role of parents. But this does not mean that the later years are unimportant – far from it. There is a discussion of the various ways in which different local education authorities have attempted to provide for talented children, and the importance of enthusiastic and dedicated teaching is underlined. But the central point of the book is that there are a number of educational principles and practices which encourage and develop children's special talents. These should be made available, as far as possible, to all our children. To quote from *Gifted or Able?*, '. . . what is good for the gifted is good for the generality of children'.

The book examines many misconceptions about the nature of giftedness, and effectively shells a number of shibboleths. It is sensible in its treatment of educational practices, pointing out the danger of 'hothousing' children, as opposed to a healthy encouragement and stimulation of their interests. It is a very readable book, enlivened with many fascinating details of the career and development of eminent individuals in many different areas of human activity. The authors, too, have hit the difficult target of writing at a level which both parent and professional will be able to enjoy.

Like Peter Young and Colin Tyre's previous title in this series, *Dyslexia or Illiteracy?*, this book offers a fresh look at an old problem. Moreover, it offers this new perspective at a most opportune time, when parents and educators are concerned as never before to improve the educational experiences that we offer our children. The purpose of this is specified clearly and unambiguously in the book's subtitle – *Realizing Children's Potential*. What better aim?

Phillip Williams

Introduction

'But Does He Play Football?'

'But does he play football?' This common reaction to hearing that a 10-year-old has excelled in chess, music or mathematics typifies society's ambivalent attitude to giftedness, genius, prodigies, the talented and those of exceptional ability, label them how we will. Parents of academically gifted girls are similarly asked, 'But what about boyfriends?' We admire prodigies but envy them because they are better than most of us. We try to put them into some acceptable construct: they must be worse than the rest of us in certain respects or doomed to die early of consumption or celibacy – or something worse.

The purpose of this book is to provide everyone concerned with education, including parents, with a clearer picture of the nature of gifted pupils and the ways of educating them. Gifted children are the subject of a number of myths which have served them and all children ill. They have been, too, the subject of controversy, exploitation and hot-housing.

The myths have concerned their nature, their intelligence, their creativity and their needs. For example: giftedness is an accident of heredity – a genetic abnormality; genius is near to madness, creativity akin to schizophrenia; the strength of one faculty is compensated by weakness in another; gifted children must have IQs of 140 or over; giftedness is a handicap; high intelligence is a simple matter of fast neural processing or good guessing; all gifted people have high IQs; gifted children all grow into happy, socially adjusted, successful adults but don't get Nobel prizes; prodigies burn out; genius is all a matter of early stimulation – it's too late

1

at eight; gifted children shouldn't be encouraged to work hard at their gifts; and there's no such thing as giftedness.

Some psychologists may eschew the term 'giftedness' and talk instead about verbal and performance intelligence quotients, convergent and divergent thinking, creativity. Some won't mention intelligence or measure IQs but will talk of higher cognitive functions. However, talented and experienced musicians, athletes, artists or mathematicians have no difficulty in talking about and identifying similarly gifted young people. They will talk readily about giftedness, sensitivity, guts, dedication, commitment, imagination, insight and the one per cent of inspiration injected into all the perspiration. Educationists may talk in terms of acceleration, creativity and enrichment. In the UK, some parents, trying to get their children settled happily in the state system, will find the greatest irony of all: their gifted children will be considered as having special needs, as if they were handicapped by some mental or sensory defect, and will be put in touch with the Local Education Authority's (LEA's) Advisory Teacher for Gifted Pupils. And they may be the lucky ones. If the children's gifts lie outside the LEA's concept of what constitutes giftedness, little if anything will be done for them. The parents will be left to manage with their own resources or to turn to some other agency for help and advice.

There is another myth, too, that being gifted academically ensures that, whatever the education provided, the gifted will succeed. In a modified form, the myth is that our educational system identifies and successfully educates the academically gifted, so why all the fuss. The truth about gifted children and their needs is infinitely more complex than this outline suggests. But because of these myths, the whole fabric of education has been distorted, complex and costly procedures have been built up to attempt to select, isolate and provide for them, and often this has been done, not in response to their needs, but for the ambitions of their parents, patrons or politicians.

Giftedness and Societies

That giftedness is politically important is most readily recognized when we think of the Olympiads for young mathematicians and scientists in the former Soviet Union, their rigorous training of dancers, gymnasts, ice-skaters and athletes, or the sudden interest in the gifted in the USA after the first Sputnik was launched. Today, in many of the major cities of the USA, pre-school children are tested to secure admission to prestigious nursery schools. Japan not only has a highly competitive and intensive state education system, it also has an extensive network of private cramming and coaching schools.

In Britain, we are often so confused about democracy and elitism, privilege and class, the open society and the Establishment, that we find it hard to discern the reality. Simple words get massaged into obfuscation. Depending on our political persuasion, we may fondly believe that we have an international reputation for the best educational system in the world as we gaze at the groves of academe in Oxbridge and in our independent public schools, or at egalitarian, unstreamed, mixed-ability, neighbourhood comprehensive schools freed from the 11 + and feeding our redbrick universities and colleges. We may believe that, for all the inequalities of our society, in which 26 per cent of all children are in families which earn less than half the average income, all children have equal opportunities to succeed and become Prime Minister.

Yet at the same time there is such concern about our educational system that we are assailed on all sides with criticism of it by politicians, industrialists, scientists, artists, trade unionists and parents. Increasingly, it is argued that our expensively educated mandarins and Establishment figures have only been half educated and are out of touch with science and technology. It has been claimed that not one of our top civil servants has a science degree, and Sir Denis Rooke, President of the British Association for the Advancement of Science, said in August 1991 that, 'The depth of ignorance of scientific affairs among some ministers is absolutely abysmal.'

Sir Claus Moser, Warden of Wadham College, Oxford, in his presidential address to the 1990 meeting of the British Association for the Advancement of Science, called for a Royal Commission on education, arguing that the percentage of UK gross domestic product devoted to education fell below that of Sweden and Denmark and the methods used by the Department of Education to predict demand for graduates was long discredited. He said, 'Wherever you touch our education system, major deficiences undermining the future of children and country emerge.' Whereas in Japan and the USA over 90 per cent of 16-year-olds are in full-time education, in Britain the figure is 50 per cent. Only 20 per cent of our 18-year-olds are in full-time education, compared with 59 per cent in Japan and 51 per cent in the USA.

There is concern, too, that a large percentage of our children who do not attend private sector or middle-class area schools are receiving a grossly inadequate education. In England and Wales, Her Majesty's Inspectorate (HMI) of Schools (DES, 1991) reported that one in five primary schools was failing to teach reading adequately, and one in twenty 10-year-olds was virtually illiterate. Other recent reports by HMI have drawn attention to the poor state of buildings, staff shortages in such key subject areas as mathematics, the sciences and music, lack of continuity of teaching in inner-city areas because of staff turnover and poor school libraries. Whereas only 9 per cent of the school population attend fee-paying independent schools, they fill 25 per cent of university places and nearly half of Oxbridge places. Half the pupils from independent schools gain two or more A levels, compared with only 14 per cent of comprehensive school pupils who gain one or more A levels. As John Rae, ex-headmaster of Westminster School, has pointed out, 'The fundamental flaw in the British education system is that it is designed to produce a well-educated elite and an under-educated majority.' In contrast, he maintained, Japan's educational system serves the national interest and is designed to produce a well-educated population for a hi-tech economy.

A survey commissioned in 1990 by the British Broadcasting Corporation (BBC), the Training Agency and the Adult Literacy and Basic Skills Unit found that over 3 million adults in Britain were unable to do simple sums using the four rules and 59 per cent could not do simple interest calculations correctly. The National Curriculum is intended to improve some aspects of this situation, although it seems to have been forgotten that we have long had the parameters of our curricula determined by examination syllabuses.

When the myths about giftedness are cleared away, when the arguments about elitism and egalitarianism are defused, we shall see more clearly that we need a much deeper and broader concept of giftedness and more rigorous social and educational policies to foster, identify and develop the panoply of talents of our children. For, in order to identify all gifted children, we must improve the education of all our children, and in order that all of them are educated to realize their full potential as our most precious resource, we need teachers qualified, trained and provided with books and equipment in small enough classes to deliver the *quality* of service which alone can transform our education system.

Parenting in a Social Setting

We are learning animals possessed of great curiosity and it is only through learning and experience that individually and as a species we realize our full potential and survive. What we have to learn in each generation grows exponentially, and what we have yet to learn – about our planet, our universe and about the universe within ourselves – is infinitely greater than all we have so far learned. Moreover, so much of what we think we know we must unlearn or modify and so much of what we know, we know is inadequate.

The explosion of learning of language, mobility, dexterity and socialization in infancy is the result of the shared social process of parenting in which the child is learning from parent and vice versa. It is the most vital, truly creative human process and the least regarded or rewarded.

From an understanding of this learning process we can build a model that elevates the process of instruction to its proper place, which will serve the most and the least able alike. But to expect an overnight revolution in our educational system is unrealistic. In order that proper provision is made for gifted pupils, we make specific proposals to guide and support parents and suggest methods to accelerate the provision of resources of staff and equipment in schools and tertiary education. Thus our aim, expressed in our subtitle, is the realization of human potential.

There is no such animal as The Gifted Child, but there are children who have different propensities and potentials from their peers because each child is unique. Gifted children dazzle us with their altruism and compassion, their insights and empathy, their mastery of techniques and disciplines, their dedication and their comprehension, their dexterities and agilities, the sounds, the shapes and colours they make, the language and languages they transform. There are many more gifted children than we know and many more children are able to attain so much more than is expected of them. We should identify them and their abilities and welcome and foster them in all their diversity. Human nature is not in the cloning business.

Overview

The education of exceptionally able children raises fundamental questions not only about the organization of education and the curriculum but about the nature of human abilities, society's values, parenting, the psychology of child development and of learning, and of the complexity of our multi-faceted personalities. Until recently, the majority of studies of giftedness have concentrated upon intelligence, intellectual abilities and creativity but, important as these aspects are, there has been a growing recognition that we need a wider and deeper conceptualization of the subject, which includes such factors as curiosity, motivation, cognitive learning strategies, abilities which are life-enhancing and strategies which are concerned with life skills and problem solving. We need to recognize differences between individuals in terms of their courage, cooperativeness and commitment, for instance, which in real life, outside test and academic situations, are now seen as of greater relevance to achievement and human survival. Above all, we need a pedagogy rigorous enough to address the realization of all our children's abilities. This we have attempted to provide in the context of current concerns about education and the needs of society and in the light of research, the lives of gifted people and our own experience.

In the first two chapters, we examine concepts of intelligence and abilities and concerns for quality and excellence in education and, in Chapter 3, discuss attitudes about provision polarized around political concepts of elitism and egalitarianism. From the results of two longitudinal studies of the academically able, it becomes apparent that we need to look both at a broader spectrum of abilities and at the ways in which children learn so much so rapidly in infancy.

In Chapters 4 and 5, we explore why the evidence points away from concerns about heredity to the importance of nurture, the key role of parents and parenting, and to early learning in the development of abilities and attitudes. The ways in which instruction leads learning and the role of mentors, coaches and tutors, together with the importance of good nursery education, and the nature and dangers of hot-housing, are examined. The importance of all-round development is emphasized. Throughout we relate theory to evidence from the lives of outstanding people and of children and young people with whom we have been privileged to work – suitably fictionalized to preserve anonymity – and deliberately present a mosaic of achievements in many spheres of human activity.

This diversity of achievement is particularly significant in Chapter 6 where we examine the nature of genius, the concept of creativity and strategies that have been recommended to develop it. Again the importance of knowledge and education appear paramount and their significance is highlighted when gender differences are examined.

The broader conceptualization of giftedness assumes importance when we examine, in Chapter 7, the nature of the savant syndrome, prodigies and those with specific abilities in athletics, leadership, caring, crafts, music, etc. The contributions they make to our understanding of giftedness and its diversity lead to the examination of educational provisions.

In Chapter 8, we examine LEA provision and studies of what parents and educationists consider best identify and realize the potential of children in the public and private sectors. Throughout our examination of the evidence, it becomes clear that what is good for the gifted is good for the generality of children and that it is only by delivering a service of the highest quality that the rich diversity of abilities of pupils can be revealed and developed.

In the concluding Chapters 9 and 10, we examine problems of giftedness and what special measures are necessary to realize the potential of the exceptionally able and of all pupils. These emphasize the importance of enthusiastic, highly qualified professional teachers, of continuity and quality control of educational provision and resources from nursery to sixth-form college, the roles of sponsorship and patronage, and the depoliticization of education by a consensual commitment to a concern for excellence and the quality of education.

CHAPTER 1

Giftedness and Intelligence

There is a popular view that, by definition, gifted children have IQs of 140 upwards and that testing intelligence by psychologists using an individually administered intelligence test, such as the Weschler Intelligence Scales for Children, the British Ability Scales or the Kaufmann Assessment Battery for Children, can help to identify children who might otherwise not present as extraordinarily able. Used in this way and in conjunction with other data, educational or clinical psychologists have often advised parents or educationists on strategies to help children realize their abilities. However, today, many psychologists have doubts about the efficacy of these tests and about the ethics of using them and there are a variety of ways in which they may satisfy themselves and others about the abilities and needs of children. Unfortunately, the terms intelligence and IQ have become such a part of language that we tend to use them as if we knew what they meant. Many readers may have found it reassuring to read the first sentence of this paragraph and think, 'Yes, now we know where we are', when, of course, we have said nothing more than that lots of people think something which may or may not be true.

When Alfred Binet, as the director of the psychology laboratory at the Sorbonne, was invited in 1904 to construct a test to identify pupils who might need special education, he reasoned that older children would perform better on mental tasks than younger children and that what was needed was a set of tasks arranged in chronological order. Children of 7 years of age who performed at the 5-year-old level, for instance, needed special help, his 'mental orthopaedics', in small classes to enable them to improve. It was all very simple, sensible and empirical. In his words, 'It

7

matters very little what the tests are so long as they are numerous.' He avoided items like reading skills, which reflected schooling or rote learning and emphasized that he was not measuring intelligence, which was too complex to be measured, and that the results of his tests were purely diagnostic and did not represent innate or immutable qualities. He fully recognized that children from cultured homes who attended schools with small classes would most likely out-perform children from poor homes educated in large classes.

Unfortunately, some psychologists here and in the USA fastened upon Binet's tests and adopted his notions for purposes he never intended and the highly profitable testing industry was quickly spawned to serve the interests of armed forces, employers and educational administrators. On the one hand, they adopted the concept of intelligence as a single human attribute like height and, on the other, they maintained that it was a faculty which was largely inherited. Some of the arguments about how much intelligence was inherited – 70 per cent, 80 per cent? – and how much environmentally determined, read like the discussions about how many angels could stand on the tip of a needle. Intelligence is an abstract quality like strength and soon psychologists realized that it might have a general factor and some special ones (Spearman, 1904) or be made up of lots of bits. In 1956, Guilford (1967), using a cube as a model, identified over 120 bits. So far as we know, no-one has used an oblate spheroid as a model, yet. In retrospect, it was like a re-run of phrenology – a book on that subject triggered Terman's interest in psychology – but at a pseudo-intellectual level.

It is also understandable that psychologists, anxious to ape physics in their embryonic 'soft' science and make it a 'hard' one, were eager to have something to measure – for, if you can't measure it, it doesn't exist. Statistics blossomed and psychologists such as Spearman, with his rank correlation coefficient, became contributors to its development and application to research methodology. The reification of intelligence as an actual entity and the ranking of individuals according to test performance still persists in some quarters, as evidenced by the Mensa Society, and, because tests have been standardized on large populations, they have many practical applications.

If one defines what is to be measured and always uses the same piece of knotted string to measure it, it is perfectly proper to compare the results, especially if one subjects them to stringent statistical analysis. But no matter how accurately one has measured, the value or significance of what has been measured may still be in doubt. Unfortunately, even measuring people's height accurately is not the simple matter it appears at first sight. How would we measure an abstract quality like strength and equate it to weight or height or age? The sensible advice we would give anyone who suggested embarking on such a project would be 'Don't': strength is an abstraction, and if you want to investigate human performance do so by studying discrete elements in specific situations. Today, it is that direction in which studies of intellect have moved, as we shall discuss later.

The proliferation of tests and of definitions of the indefinable abstract noun 'intelligence' are two of the more banal manifestations of the attempt to make psychology a hard science and put it to practical use. Some of the more widely used definitions of intelligence include:

- The ability to deal with new situations.
- The ability to see relationships, including complex and abstract ones.
- The ability to learn and to apply what has been learnt to new situations.
- The capacity to inhibit instinctive behaviour and, in the light of experience, behave advantageously as a social individual.
- The ability to handle complex stimuli.
- The ability to respond quickly to information.
- A group of mental processes involving perception, association, memory, reasoning, imagination.

One of the more unpopular aspects of the 11 + selection was the use of intelligence tests, but what caused the greatest controversy was the suggestion, which repeatedly kept surfacing, that there was a difference in the intelligence levels of races (Jensen, 1969; Eysenck, 1971, 1973) and social classes. This was not because the mean IQ of Japanese was said to be 106, and that of Japanese children 111, compared with the mean WASP (White Anglo-Saxon Protestant) IQ of 100, which is something which might have upset the testers, but because the racist implications upset black Americans and democratic public opinion generally.

From the outset, Sir Francis Galton (1869), the genius who studied genius, had argued that intelligence is inherited and throughout the history of psychology there has been the influence of the eugenics movement he and his follower, Karl Pearson, founded. There are, of course, fundamental genetic, moral, philosophical, ethical and political objections to eugenics. In its positive form, it advocates improving the race by selective breeding, as Hitler encouraged Nordic types to breed; in its negative form, by 'removing the unfit', it resulted in the holocaust.

In the USA, H.H. Goddard (1914) used Binet to construct scales of mental deficiency and to support his views on the social stratification of society, and on controlling breeding and immigration to protect society and arrive at a democracy which was a 'truly benevolent aristocracy'. Terman (1916) wanted his tests to be used universally to weed out 'high-grade mental defectives', like 12-year-olds with reading ages of 7 years.

Terman's advocacy of testing and of its evidence of the innateness of intelligence and, therefore, of class differences in ability, as we shall see later, flawed the research design of his monumental study of gifted pupils in 1947.

In this country, Galton was a patient of Dr Burt and supported his son, Cyril, later Sir Cyril Burt, who had also studied under Karl Pearson, in his early career as a psychologist. To the end of his days, Burt maintained his eugenicist's beliefs, arguing that intelligence was inherited and that both genetically and environmentally the working classes were inferior. As if the obscenities of Nazism's adoption of eugenic principles had never existed, he wrote: 'The over-all efficiency of the citizens who make up a nation or a state must in the last resort depend on what has been called its "chromosomal pool". Improved environmental amenities can of themselves ensure no lasting results; but changes in a nation's genetic constitution are likely to be irreversible' (Burt, 1958).

When it came to selection for grammar school, Burt, doyen of British psychologists and the first psychologist to be appointed to an LEA, London, advocated the use of intelligence tests which he thought better employed to identify the able than the weak-minded. However, he then extended his concept of innate intelligence to innate differences of temperament, self-discipline and social responsibility between social classes. Why educate the working-class scholarship boys who 'frequently fail to stay the course; by the time they are sixteen the attractions of high wages and of cheap entertainment during leisure hours prove stronger than their desire for further knowledge and skill'? He suspected, 'an innate and transmissable difference of temperamental stability and in character, or in the neurophysiological basis on which such temperamental and moral differences tend to be built up'. Naturally, he covered himself by stating that there was a pressing need for more extensive research. The trouble with Burt, we suspect, was that he always knew in advance what he wanted to find and, in consequence, only saw what he was looking for. Yet he was an intelligent and erudite man who certainly paid his debt to Galton and, as we shall see later, lived to recognize some of the inadequacies of the psychometrics he had promoted.

With this sort of provenance it is not surprising, therefore, that the use of intelligence tests has declined and that in some US states their use is banned. There is another important reason why IQ tests have waned in popularity: even if they test abilities of one sort or another, which undoubtedly many of them do, they do not test life-skills, such as personality, motivational and emotional factors, which may crucially affect future performance and achievement. Attempts have been made to construct test which are 'culture-free' and which measure this unitary intelligence untrammelled by the effects of environment and differences of class and society. One of the more simplistic notions currently being investigated is that of measuring cerebral reaction times using electro-encephalograms, a method that can be used with infants and young children. Will parents of 'slow' babies blame heredity or one another, or their doctors or nurses or perinatal factors and sue accordingly?

We will discuss concepts of intellect in relation to giftedness later but here we would suggest that taken alone, the result of an IQ test has little value and the view of a unitary, innate faculty such as intelligence diverts our attention from the diversity of abilities, skills and qualities of children. Again, if we are told, for instance, that children are highly intelligent but are grossly underperforming, what is significant is not their abilities but the factors which have caused their inability to perform, factors we should have been attending to all along. IQ tests are unlikely to have discovered why Churchill or Einstein were underperforming at school, if such was in fact the case, nor could they have predicted how they would develop. And we all know people who are intelligent but can do nothing, all empty words and vain gestures.

Instead of assessing children's intelligence as measured by intelligence tests, we would be better employed finding out what they can do and how well and quickly they can learn to do more. Tests of intelligence, sometimes masquerading as tests of mental ability, usually succeed in testing what they have been designed to test. But many have a strong verbal element which favours children with a highly verbal background, as, for example, the chattering yuppies of yesteryear, and children of professional people. They will not identify children with artistic or musical abilities and they are unlikely to reveal pupils of exceptional mathematical ability. Some sensitive or over-anxious children may underperform in test situations, and some exceptionally gifted children may find the questions so banal that they will suspect a trick and spend time searching for hidden meanings. As one child commented, when asked if he'd enjoyed the test, 'All right, but if I'd wanted to find out how smart I was I would have asked better questions.' There was, too, the boy who performed brilliantly when tested and, when asked why he thought he didn't do better in school, replied with disarming frankness and truth, 'Oh, that's because basically I'm lazy, like my dad' – another hereditarian.

Growing dissatisfaction with the concept of intelligence and the failure of American education to produce spacecraft led to a return to another of Galton's preoccupations. Galton wondered how people could associate freely, dream differently and could dredge up from their minds seemingly disparate ideas which they could then relate to one another. In the 1960s, creativity (Torrance, 1962) was thought to be what distinguished the genius or exceptionally able. Maybe we could teach creativity and catch up with the Russian spacemen, produce more Einsteins or destroy more territory more quickly. There were even attempts to construct tests of creativity, but this proved more difficult than the Trivial Pursuits approach to intelligence testing. The subject, however, did focus attention away from the nature–nurture debate and upon a number of important aspects of human abilities, such as problem solving, which we will examine in detail later.

Two strands have emerged from these preoccupations with intelligence and creativity which do have a bearing upon our central concern for the development of the potential of all our children's multifarious abilities. On the one hand, there has grown up a more scientific and analytic approach to the house of intellect, the cognitive and creative functions of the mind and its biochemistry. On the other, and no less important, is the realization that motivational factors – including arousal levels which affect curiosity, the emotional, impulse-driven or conative aspects of personality – and differences in persistence, courage, together with sensitivity to environmental influences of a moral, ethical, philosophical or cultural nature, all have a bearing on performance through the personal constructs we build in our minds of ourselves and of reality.

These last aspects of development are of vital concern and need to be an integral part of the content of education. The quality of education, whether in science or the arts, must be informed by a concern for truth, rationality and logic, for values which are life-enhancing and which put concern for others, social responsibility and cooperation above confrontation, greed, casuistry and chauvinism. Increasingly, young people have demonstrated in China, Czechoslovakia, the USSR and South Africa, for example, that they reject oppression, propaganda and double standards. Education has a responsibility to transmit values, qualities and standards as an integral part of our culture. It must cultivate the minds of all pupils to think for themselves, to exercise judgement and discretion, to apply standards and values and their critical faculties. Intelligence without knowledge is useless. Creativity without culture is barren. A curriculum without values is valueless.

The House of Intellect

Naturalistic models of the mind have reflected the ability of human beings to visualize their world. The more able we have become at distinguishing the complexity of our universe, the better we have been able to conceptualize our minds and see ourselves as part of an ecological system and rescue our brains from mind–body dualism. The Greeks understood well enough the performance of puppets and saw behaviour as the pulling of strings (neurons). In the sixteenth century, vapours and the spleen were responsible for differences of personality. Descartes visualized a hydraulics system operating in the tubes of our nerves. Guilford saw intelligence as a block of cubes.

Today, we have moved away from the telephone exchange to computer models of the brain. While the latter have helped conceptualize some aspects of cognition and the use of heuristic and artificial intelligence (AI) studies, foreshadowed by Alan Turing (1937), have illuminated an understanding of processes within the 'black box' of the brain, the model we now need to develop is a biochemical one. Computer models reflect only what we think we know about thought and the programs we feed in are therefore limited to those algorithms. The British cybernetrician, Gordon Pask, in his *The Cybernetics of Human Learning and Performance* (1975), anticipates this in his distinction, in biologically self-replicating systems, between M-Individuals (mechanically characterized individuals) and P-Individuals (psychologically characterized individuals). The difference between the computer and what Marvin Minsky eloquently called 'the meat machine' of the brain is that the meat is an active learner, pre-programmed to survive, with its own fuzzy logic. Undoubtedly, the more that brilliant minds address themselves to studying the processes of more and more complex computers, designed to think more elaborately for themselves, the better we shall understand thought processes. But those designs must take on board advances in neuropsychology (Luria, 1972) and our understanding of the interaction of the deep structures of the brain, the limbic system, the posterior cerebral hemisphere processing sensory input and the frontal and pre-frontal areas which retain, plan and control.

They must also consider the complex biochemistry of the brain with its constant consumption of calories to produce the tens of thousands of proteins needed to maintain the electrical potential and interconnection between its 100 billion neurons whether we are at rest, engaged in physical or mental activity, or asleep. From birth the brain is being modified and is sufficiently plastic for some time to adapt to experience, to external stimuli. Throughout our lives, memory traces are transmitted and migrate to be stored away, and are often seemingly extinguished only to be triggered back to conscious recall by a chance event. The network of connections is constantly being modified, internally by hormonal and other changes as the individual develops, and externally by learning from experience. Instead of each individual being formed by inexorable genetic processes, we can see more clearly how each unique chance combination of genes in the neonate is in turn uniquely modified by experience.

Colin Blakemore (1988) puts it in these words:

> The brain is built by instructions in the genes, but modified by events throughout life, from the uterus to the death-bed. In those terms our

actions are the combined results of the information that constantly bombards the senses, of the stored memories of past events, of desires and ambitions (partly inherent, partly learned), of childhood experiences captured in their effect on the structure of the brain, of the education that we have received, of our knowledge of conventions of right and wrong and, indeed, of our understanding of the existence of courts and methods of punishment.

It is this concept of the modification of inherited characteristics which we need in order to understand the diversity of abilities and the ways in which they may manifest themselves and be developed. Belief in a unitary intelligence or specific gifts for flute- or rugby-playing or vitamin tablets to increase ability are notions too simplistic to do justice to the potential of children in all their variety.

Thinking about Thinking about Learning

Guilford's model of 120 + elementary abilities and Vernon's (1971) hierarchy of abilities – *general, verbal–educational, practical–mechanical, minor* and *specific abilities* – are examples of attempts to analyse functions. Sternberg (1979), using an information-processing model, identifies five ways in which we think or process information: *metacomponents* for higher-order planning, problem solving and decision making; *performance components* for carrying out the problem solving: *acquisition components* for learning; *retention components* for recalling what we already know; and *transfer components* for generalizing from one task to another. Howard Gardner (1983) proposes six abilities or components of 'multiple intelligence': *linguistic, logical–mathematical, spatial, musical, bodily–kinaesthetic* and *personal*. This represents a useful conceptualization of some of the kinds of abilities observed in the generality of people, in gifted individuals and the idiots savants alike. They are abilities all may have to a modest degree at different levels, which some may have to a marked degree and which others may have in isolation. We have moved a long way from a monotypic view of intelligence. 'Spectrum' tests devised by Gardner and his colleagues for pre-school children identify 15 specific types of ability. But they recognize they could have selected many more.

When we identify abilities we naturally select those which we *think* are most valuable. Innuit culture depends on the ability of people to distinguish between many varieties of ice and to be manually dexterous. Aborigines in Australia needed the ability to follow tracks which are indiscernible to white people. Street-sharp children, like gamblers, invent their own computational systems. All children are born with the ability to learn language, whatever language or languages they happen to be bathed in. Barbara Rogoff and her colleagues (1984) have looked at these cultural factors in different societies, such as the Navajo and African peoples, and the ways in which they influence child development and conclude:

> A major contribution that cross-cultural research and theorizing have made to developmental psychology is the notion that the meaningfulness of the materials, demands, goals, and social situation of an activity channels an individual's performance on a task. Sociocultural experience and individual functioning are fundamentally tied to one another and are, thus, companions in human behaviour and development.

Not only is the child able to adapt to the experience to which she or he may be exposed in a specific culture, parents select those experiences, say language, which they consider will be most advantageous for the child. In Rogoff's words:

> . . . children adapt their cognitive and social skills to the particular demands of their culture through practice in particular activities. Children learn to use physical and conceptual tools provided by the culture to handle the problems of importance in routine activities, and they rely on more experienced members of the culture to guide their development.

The great diversity of language and of cultures to which children can adapt is evidence of the plasticity and adaptability of their brains, of learning in a social setting, of becoming able and growing in intelligence. When we consider children's abilities, therefore, we need to look beyond the narrow confines of unitary views of intelligence, deterministic views of inheritance and, too, beyond a 'back to basics' and examination-dominated curriculum, important though that may be, to the enormous variety of skills and activities our multifaceted culture depends upon. This may encourage us to discern in our children abilities such as tenacity or empathy, social skills which Sternberg and Davidson (1985) call niche-fitting skills, and gifts like manual dexterity, curiosity or a sense of the absurd, which we have previously ignored or underestimated. We may, too, wish to place abilities in a new hierarchical order. Finally, we may wish to accelerate and to enrich the education of children and give them a greater variety of role models, more opportunities to learn by imitation or to have concrete experiences before being expected to acquire abstract reasoning.

Able or Gifted?

So far, we have used the term 'gifted' as a flag of convenience: an every-day word with an everyday use. Whilst we do not consider that children are born with specific gifts, we do believe that it is entirely correct to say that children are born with a variety of general and specific abilities: that is a part of being human and of each and every one of us being unique and uniquely different. We also believe that some children are born with propensities which, given appropriate encouragement and instruction, enable them to acquire skills of a high order more rapidly than the generality of children. They may learn some skills, like shuffling cards, holding a bow, perceiving harmony, distinguishing the hues of colours or telling a story, more readily than others. They may have more efficient memories for words or music or shapes. They may be more patient, forebearing, empathetic and caring than the majority. Where these propensities are combined with the ability to learn from experience and that experience is in harmony with their needs and development, some children may well manifest abilities which are outstanding when compared with the great majority of other children. Such children present as being exceptionally able. Exceptionally able athletes, writers, mathematicians, chess players, mimics, raconteurs, naturalists, gymnasts, tap-dancers, cellists or contortionists may be said to be gifted. We see no reason to dispense with such an all-purpose term. Examining how abilities or propensities become exceptional abilities or gifts is what we are about.

A Check on Checklists

In order to help teachers identify gifted pupils, it has frequently been suggested that checklists of their characteristics should be used. Not suprisingly, checklists reflect the definitions of giftedness adhered to by their designers or attempt to be so all-embracing in their desire that no likely candidate be excluded that they end up by including everyone. One of the earliest (Laycock, 1957) and most widely used is clearly designed to identify high academic ability and its 20 items cover most of the points teachers might subsume under their heading of 'a bright child':

Laycock's checklist for teachers
1. Possess superior powers of reasoning, of dealing with abstractions, of generalizing from specific facts, of understanding meanings, and of seeing relationships.
2. Have great intellectual curiosity.
3. Learn easily and readily.
4. Have a wide range of interests.
5. Have a broad attention-span that enables them to concentrate on, and persevere in solving problems and pursuing interests.
6. Are superior in the quantity and quality of vocabulary as compared with other children of their own age.

7. Have ability to do effective work independently.
8. Have learned to read early (often well before school age).
9. Exhibit keen powers of observation.
10. Show initiative and originality in intellectual work.
11. Show alertness and quick response to new ideas.
12. Are able to memorize quickly.
13. Have great interest in the nature of man and the universe (problems of origin and destiny, etc).
14. Possess unusual imagination.
15. Follow complex directions easily.
16. Are rapid readers.
17. Have several hobbies.
18. Have reading interests which cover a wide range of subjects.
19. Make frequent and effective use of the library.
20. Are superior in arithmetic, particularly in problem solving.

It has a strong emphasis on literacy and any child who exhibits most of its characteristics is likely to perform well at school, and already be regarded by teachers as able. What might be doubted is whether such paragons are gifted. Might they not be above-average children from 'good homes'? It would be a simple matter to reduce these items by half and identify academically able children and still miss all the musically, athletically, artistically and otherwise gifted ones.

We can contrast Laycock's checklist with the following list of creative competences, which Parker (1989) considers, along with cognitive abilities and affective abilities, relevant to giftedness in art and which 'fit easily into the four basic components of creativity cited for many years by Guilford, Torrance, Williams, and countless others':

1. **Fluency**
   a. Expressiveness
   b. Spontaneous flow of ideas
   c. Lengthy periods spent on problem finding and solution
2. **Flexibility**
   a. Tendency to experiment freely with a variety of ideas and subjects, media, materials and techniques
   b. Facility for solving problems using nontraditional methods
   c. Aptitude for viewing/approaching art from a different perspective
   d. Tolerance of ambiguity and conflict
   e. Ability to adapt from one situation or medium to another
3. **Originality**
   a. High degree of imagination; ability to image clearly
   b. Freedom from stimuli
   c. Tendency to experiment with problem finding as opposed to adopting preconceived problem situations

4. Elaboration
   a. Use of many elements
   b. Facility for piggybacking/hitchhiking on (as opposed to copying) the ideas of others

We introduced this characterization of creativity at this point because it also highlights the reliance researchers place on it when they tackle the problem of identifying gifted children who do not come from middle-class, highly verbal and literate homes, which have got them reading well before school.

Sisk (1988), discussing the major problems in urban inner-city schools in the USA, argues that there is not only a reluctance on the part of educationists and parents alike to recognize that giftedness can exist in lower-class populations but that disadvantaged pupils, because of language and other factors, will have difficulty in performing well on tests and, if gifted, may find themselves attending schools where the programmes concentrate on compensatory education for cultural disadvantage. She maintains that it becomes important, therefore, to view their positive traits and use these as a general screening device and as a viable part of a comprehensive identification procedure. Her checklist identifies the following characteristics:

- High mathematical ability
- Alert curiosity
- Independence of action
- Initiative, anxious to do new things
- Fluency in nonverbal communication
- Imagination in thinking
- Learning quickly through experience
- Retaining and using ideas and information well
- Showing a desire to learn in daily work
- Originality and creativity in thinking
- Varied interests
- Responding well to visual media
- Ability to generalize learning to other areas and to show relationships among apparently unrelated ideas
- Resourceful, ability to solve problems by ingenious methods
- Imaginative storytelling, language rich in imagery
- Mature sense of humour
- Responsive to the concrete

The majority of checklists derive from research into intelligence and creativity but they have rarely been tested in the classroom for their validity. This is not to deny that they may not prove useful but to question how much reliability may be placed upon their predictive value.

Sisk, rightly, describes a number of other measures teachers may use to identify these pupils.

A further difficulty with such checklists is that they tend to confirm teachers' own estimations of their pupils' abilities and, therefore, are unlikely to yield the results for which they were originally designed. They rarely identify pupils who may be deliberately underperforming; they are not useful in identifying under-achievers because of lack of opportunity and, of course, they are narrowly concerned with intellectual and creative abilities. The Essex Curriculum Extension Project has addressed itself in its booklet *Identifying the Gifted Child* (1985) to the problem of under-achievers. In addition to reviewing identification strategies such as pupil's developmental history, teacher observation, checklists, standardized tests and their recording, it provides a checklist of characteristics of exceptionally able pupils, drawn up by 90 experienced teachers from their own observations. This, in addition to most of the items included in the previous lists, includes such items as 'Asks many provocative searching questions', 'Listens only to part of the explanation', 'Criticises constructively', 'Is unwilling to accept authoritarian pronouncements without critical examination', 'Day dreams', 'Shows empathy towards others'.

'The Under-Achiever: A check-list of characteristics', taken from *Teaching Bright Pupils* (Nottingham University School of Education) lists the following:

- Anti-school
- Orally good while written work poor
- Apparently bored
- Restless and inattentive
- Absorbed in a private world
- Tactless and impatient with slower minds
- Friendly with older pupils
- Self-critical
- Poor social relations with peers and teachers
- Emotionally unstable
- Outwardly self-sufficient

BUT ALSO

- Creative when motivated
- Quick to learn
- Able to solve problems
- Able to ask provocative questions
- Persevering when motivated
- Given to abstract thought
- Inventive in response to open-ended questions

Very few studies exist which examine the effectiveness and reliability of checklists. One question teachers may well ask is whether or not all the items have the same weight and how many can be ignored before the test is considered to give a negative indication. Renzulli and Hartman's (1971) 'Scale for Rating Behavioural Characteristics of Superior Students' is, perhaps, the most soundly constructed and contains four sub-scales – learning, motivational, creativity and leadership characteristics – ratings which are highly correlated with one another and with other objective measures of the characteristics.

Denton and Postlethwaite (1985), whose work in Oxfordshire was concerned with identifying able pupils in the classroom and which we examine in depth in Chapter 8, distinguished between these general checklists and the subject-specific checklists that they drew up and which, they considered, subject specialists could draw up as *guides* to draw attention to pupils' characteristics which might not be reflected in pupil records, examination results and from working with the children in the classroom. They rightly wished to base their checklists upon items which had been validated by research, but only in the case of mathematics was this possible. For mathematics, they used Krutetskii's (1976) research, which identified the characteristics of pupils with high mathematical potential, and compiled a checklist based on it and their own background work, each item of which they then validated. This was done by devising separate tests for each item which were administered to a group of pupils of moderate mathematical ability and a group of known high mathematical ability. Their checklists for the other subjects – English, French and Physics – were made by reviewing the literature of the subjects to identify significant characteristics and by discussions with teachers. The checklists were only used as guides for teachers and no claims were made for their validity.

We are convinced that this is the direction in which identification of pupils' abilities must go. If teachers need lists of generalized characteristics to identify gifted pupils, then, clearly, they do not know their pupils and are in no position to respond adequately to the lists. And, if the lists have no or little proven validity or predictive value, teachers would be better employed getting to know their pupils by teaching them. What limited use the checklists have is, perhaps, in helping to sensitize teachers to general characteristics of able pupils.

With the implementation of the National Curriculum and Standard Assessment Tasks (SATs), it will be increasingly possible, as teachers become more familiar with them, to identify those pupils who are performing markedly ahead of their peers. The danger will be that gifted pupils may be held back or that they will not be extended because of low expectations. Subject teachers who know their pupils will always have a vital part to play by enthusing and motivating them and, in the process, identifying those of outstanding ability who can go 'beyond the information given'. So far as school subjects are concerned, it is here that the main thrust of identification and development of giftedness is made and can be made. While we may urge a wider concept of giftedness extending far beyond the confines of the National Curriculum, this is not to deny the central importance of the identification and realization of potential within those subjects. One way in which teachers can extend their knowledge of pupils' abilities lies outside the curriculum; the other lies within the teaching process itself.

Beyond the Curriculum

> Leslie is a spastic quadriplegic with a speech defect who staggers around school with difficulty but finds the academic work within his grasp apart from the difficulty of writing. He is regarded as of average ability with special needs in speech and manual dexterity. A lap-top has proved a boon. His housemaster is surprised at how popular Leslie is but it is some time before he discovers why. Not only is Leslie a fine mimic – his repertoire extends way beyond the staff to a bill of celebrities – he is also a raconteur with impeccable timing and ambitions to perform on television. He writes his own material, which he rehearses in front of a mirror until he has eliminated all trace of his handicaps. His mirror-image is another persona, in fact many personae. It is only when the housemaster discovers this that the school sees Leslie as the complex and talented person he really is and begins to educate him accordingly.

In inner-city schools, teachers recognize the children who are 'street-sharp'. They may be poor at arithmetic but they can give change with speed and accuracy in their weekend market jobs or calculate betting odds faster than their teachers. In the USA, Sisk (1988) describes the attempts which have been made to develop culturally biased tests (Bruch, 1973; Meeker, 1978), which are deliberately weighted in favour of those skills, such as spatial relationships, logical reasoning, musical abilities and memory, in which black, Navajos and Mexican pupils are not disadvantaged or may excel.

In other words, if we are concerned with identifying giftedness, we should look at how children perform in their peer groups and in their own social milieu. Like Paolo Freire, we must adapt our educational methods to the social and cultural settings in which our pupils live so that they can combine their spontaneously formed concepts and procedures, learned in their social setting, with those of their teachers. We may then find that they exhibit skills and propensities which are not revealed in the classroom. In some cases, this will enable us to create new opportunities for them to achieve in school. In some cases, it may encourage schools to raise their expectations of them; in others, by recognizing and facilitating the activities in which they realize their potential outside school, we may be able to make education more relevant for them. The children who are said to be lacking in concentration in school and, in consequence are under-achieving, are often those who are seen to be patiently fishing or are absorbed in computer or other games at weekends.

Certainly, we need to be aware that the number of West Indian, Asian, inner-city area and working-class pupils who are identified as gifted is far below what one would expect having regard to the size of the populations involved. Yet we only have to visit a sports stadium to discover that the reverse is often true. The determination, discipline, dedication and abilities they demonstrate are rarely harnessed or recognized and rewarded in schools, which are only interested in a narrow range of academic skills and conformist values and are neither timetabled nor staffed to provide a properly balanced physical education curriculum. This is not the case in schools such as those described in the National Association for Gifted Children (NAGC) Survey (see Chapter 8), in which the pursuit of excellence, the emphasis on quality of education and the variety of opportunities for achievement in a diverse range of activities, are of paramount importance. As we have seen, giftedness is not something which can be measured by IQ tests or checklists, and it is in the area of life-skills, survival skills and life-enhancing abilities that we need to look for pupils of high abilities and potential. We can look more closely and insightfully within the subject areas of the curriculum and extra-curricular activities of the school and we should also look at all those activities in which pupils engage outside school, the clubs and organizations to which they belong, their interests and hobbies, for signs of abilities not revealed and harnessed in school.

CHAPTER 2

Needs are not Enough

Three Solutions

Janet read fluently at three and enjoyed Latin and French at her prep school. Her parents decided she needed the best possible education for girls and placed her at the Cheltenham Ladies College where it is already clear she will go up to Oxford. The fees and extras last year left no change out of £10 000. Janet is happy and her parents agree they are getting value for money. Her mother points out it would have been cheaper to put a boy through Eton. But it costs the LEA much more to send a child to a residential special school for children with behavioural problems.

Salman read early, too, and in his Junior School was known as Number Cruncher. His popularity in the local Comprehensive School was the result of his captaincy of the hockey team and his easy manner. Outstanding in mathematics and physics he is determined to go up to Cambridge. His Head is sure he will. His father works in a local garment factory and his mother speaks little English. Salman will qualify for a full grant and he will sell the computer software business he set up when he was 15.

Martin didn't read until he was seven when he became a voracious reader with no interest in school work although he always did comparatively well in tests and exams. He idled away his time in first and middle schools and at 9 was referred to the Educational Psychologist because of his disruptive behaviour. His WISC-R revealed a quotient of 150 verbal and 137 performance. Martin said he found school boring and the work so easy it was a waste of time doing it. His parents said they couldn't understand why he was so difficult at home and at school as they had always given him everything he wanted. He was recommended for under-age transfer to a comprehensive school with high academic standards where he excelled after some initial disciplinary problems were sorted out.

These case histories represent the three main approaches to the provision of education for gifted children in England. Those who can afford to, send their children to independent schools of their choice and provide individual tuition for talents such as music and ballet. The majority of people believe that the gifted, being gifted, would be catered for by grammar schools, sixth-form colleges or their neighbourhood comprehensive schools as an academic elite. An increasingly vocal minority believe that gifted pupils need special provision if they are to realize their potential. Prior to the 1980 Education Act, it was often argued that they were, in fact, handicapped by their giftedness. Aided by some understanding LEAs, provision was made for a small number of gifted children to attend independent schools and choir schools, anticipating the government's Assisted Places Scheme, by classifying them as in need of special education. Acceleration through the educational system, as in Martin's case, was sometimes recommended. Some LEAs followed the example of Essex and encouraged enrichment of the curriculum and Holiday Schools for gifted children.

The introduction of comprehensive education nationally, with government Circular 10/65 requiring all LEAs to draw up plans for its organization, increased many parents' concern for their academically able children. Although the abolition of the 11 + was welcomed, many saw the disappearance of the grammar schools as the removal of opportunity for the academic elite. Neighbourhood schools often meant WYLIWYG – Where You Live Is What You Get – as estate agents realized. What you got in Cardiganshire or Conservative but comprehensive Leicestershire was a world away from what you got for your children in West Ham or West Bromwich. Differences of educational provision had little to do with ability but everything to do with social class, sex and geography as one of the advocates of comprehensive schools, Professor Brian Simon, trenchantly pointed out at the time: '. . . the Cardiganshire middle-class boy has roughly one hundred and sixty times as much chance of reaching full-time higher education than the West Ham working class girl; and this when a country has, in a formal sense, committed itself to a policy of equality of opportunity'. Attempts to redress this imbalance were attacked as egalitarian, mixed-ability classes were particularly criticized and the Black Papers of 1969 were symptomatic of disquiet about so-called progressive education.

Not surprisingly, therefore, when the Warnock Committee of Inquiry into the educational provision in England, Scotland and Wales for children and young people handicapped by disabilities of body or mind, met from 1974–78, it received a body of evidence from various organizations and individuals, including parents, who urged that the needs of gifted pupils warranted the Committee's consideration. The Committee's Report, *Special Educational Needs* (DES, 1978), has been criticized for failing to address this subject. Quite properly, however, the Committee decided that 'we did not regard the problems of highly gifted children as falling within our remit, except insofar as these problems may result in emotional or behavioural disorders similar in effect to the problems of other children with whom we are concerned'. As the Committee's remit was exclusively concerned with those 'handicapped by disabilities of body or mind' it would not have been sensible to include those with gifted bodies or minds. The Report did draw attention to the DES HMI Series discussion document *Gifted Children in Middle and Comprehensive Schools* (DES, 1977) and also urged that, in initial training, teachers should be helped to understand the variety of reasons why individual children may behave in a disruptive manner, 'for example tensions in the family, school or community or the frustrations of a highly gifted child whose abilities are insufficiently recognized and developed'.

Although this was not the outcome for which the gifted lobby had hoped, following the recommendations of the Report, the Education Act 1980 abolished categorization by handicap, substituted the concept of needs and it is now within this framework that LEAs may statement gifted pupils. Many parents, supported by psychologists' reports, argue that their gifted children's needs are not being met. This is often hard to demonstrate, let alone prove, especially if their performance in school tests compares favourably with that of their peers, unless the children's plight has been allowed to deteriorate until they demonstrate disruptive or other inappropriate behaviours.

Some parents have set great store on the Education Reform Act 1988 with its opportunities for greater parental involvement, greater school autonomy, provision for opting out of LEA jurisdiction and on the National Curriculum and its levels of attainment and Standard Assessment Tasks (SATs). Others, with the money to do so, have already moved their children into private, independent education or moved to areas where standards and facilities for their gifted children are already available. Despite the recession and rising fees, in January 1991 the Independent Schools Information Service (ISIS) reported that 475 000 children were being educated privately. Pupil–staff ratios were just over 11:1. There are still independent grammar schools, such as Manchester, Portsmouth and Wolverhampton, although they now provide education for only 3 per cent of secondary pupils.

The Assisted Places Scheme, enabling bright children to attend independent secondary schools which their parents would not be able to afford, provides for about 30 000 pupils, approximately 40 per cent of whom get all of their fees paid. However, research funded by the Economic and Social Research Council (ESRC: Edwards *et al.*, 1990) found that most of the pupils so helped were from middle-class backgrounds and fewer than 10 per cent were from working-class or culturally deprived backgrounds. As the researchers conclude: 'The scheme seems to have been yet another example of an educational reform targeted towards the working class but mainly benefiting children from middle-class homes.'

Already it is clear that articulate and informed parents are taking the initiative and leading the movement for schools opting out. As advantageous as this will be for the middle-class and upwardly mobile areas, the disadvantages will be experienced in those schools remaining in LEAs. Other parents are being helped by organizations such as the National Association for Gifted Children, Mensa and its Foundation for Gifted Children, and by the European Council for High Ability and the schools for gifted, high-ability children which they have established.

But there is no national policy for gifted pupils and provision for identifying them and meeting their needs is patchy both between and within LEAs. Moreover, we have so far only considered the needs of those children whose exceptional abilities are academic. Those who are gifted in music, dance, drama, art, athletics and in so many other ways have not been considered. Nor have we considered the problems of identifying, evaluating and assessing giftedness. Today there is no longer a consensus among psychologists about the ethics of administering IQ tests or about their value, yet for many people a high IQ is the cornerstone of their concept of giftedness. In the words of Serebriakoff (1990), 'The objective standardised IQ test which has been statistically validated on large samples is fairer than any other means of judging educational potential.' We examine this question in Chapter 8.

Needs: A Deficit Model

Finally, although it may at present be expedient for parents and LEAs to resort to it, it is our considered view that the concept of special educational needs is inappropriate to the education of the gifted and to the realization of our children's potential. Special educational needs is a deficit model. It is a concept rightly concerned with enabling those children with disabilities and handicaps to access the curriculum. Gifted people are not handicapped and to regard them as such is a contradiction in terms, unless, of course, like Christy Brown they are both gifted and handicapped. Christy Brown was handicapped by cerebral palsy and, in that respect, had special educational, social and other needs. But he was gifted in his command of language and by his sense of humour, his courage and determination.

Gifted children have assets, not deficits: the deficits may be in their environment, in their parenting, in their social circumstances, in their education. Whereas handicapped pupils, including those who are gifted, may need help in learning to be mobile or in making notes or in hearing, seeing or understanding what they need to learn, gifted pupils, including those who are handicapped, want an education appropriate to their abilities. The handicapped have intrinsive deficits, the gifted may have extrinsic deficits. For this reason, we need to look at our aims of education and its process. Here the Warnock Report's goals for education are also inappropriate.

The Warnock Report's (DES, 1978) two-fold goals are essentially basic:

> They are, first, to enlarge a child's knowledge, experience and imaginative understanding, and thus his awareness of moral values and capacity for enjoyment; and secondly, to enable him to enter the world after formal education is over as an active participant in society and a responsible contributor to it, capable of achieving as much independence as possible.

There is nothing here of children's rights to participate in, and contribute to, their cultural heritage. There is no mention here of children's rights to the development of their abilities and sensibilities, nothing of honing their intellectual faculties, their curiosity, critical faculties, their discernment of values and of worthwhileness.

Whilst it might be argued that the above are subsumed by the goals, they could also be interpreted as basic criteria for the passive recipients of improving instruction designed to produce compliant consumers or the willing and contented drones of a totalitarian state. There is nothing here about excellence or of quality. This is the kind of minimal prescription for secondary school education as being for 'the hewers of wood and the drawers of water'. What all children need is the fullest possible development of all their abilities and all have a right, so far as they are able, to benefit from the culture they have inherited.

CHAPTER 3

Elitism or Egalitarianism: A False Dichotomy

If we can find for this long course of training and study men who are at all points sound of limb and sound of mind, justice will have no fault to find with us and we shall ensure the safety of our commonwealth and its institutions.

(Plato).

All men are born equal and with the same aptitudes: education alone makes the differences.

(Helvetius).

It is inevitable that, whenever the education of the gifted is discussed, the question of elitism is raised. Why should children who are clearly advantaged by being talented be further favoured by being educated in independent schools or sixth-form colleges? Should not all children be given the same education in mixed-ability classes and private education be abolished? Why should gifted pupils be allowed to skip classes and enter university at 12? Why should able children not be held back in lock-step with their less able peers? In a society which likes to think of itself as democratic, as an open society in which all enjoy equal opportunities, anything which smacks of elitism is suspect. Yet the same people who would inveigh against selection in education accept it in sport as readily as they accept it in medicine or entertainment. Behind the concept of democracy is the rejection of a ruling elite, in Pareto's sense, in which those who enjoy the benefits of birth, wealth, power and privilege become a governing elite.

The complex economic, political and class aspects of this problem are not our concern here. To deny that power elites and cultural elites exist in Western democracies – our own included – would be to deny the obvious, just as it would be folly to ignore the existence of constraints and limitations upon them. The Apostles of Cambridge are seen as a malevolent elite when they penetrate security and the Queen's aesthetic advisers with communists, but when members of the same club and their wives, such as Leonard and Virginia Woolf, Maynard Keynes and Clive Bell – the latter an elitist if ever there was one – are founders of the Bloomsbury Group and authors of economic and cultural policy, they are almost universally acclaimed. But when the rich get richer and the poor get poorer, when the hopeless take to the streets, when the obscenities of infant mortality figures outrage public decency, there are ways in which the electorate can influence policies directly and the uncaring made to care and reflect upon 'this funny old world'. Democratic rights, for all their limitations, such as the absence of a Freedom of Information Bill in the UK, protect the individual and society from the worst excesses of the judiciary, the police, politicians or the breakdown of ethics in self-regulating bodies such as banks and brokers.

But the question of elitism and egalitarianism in education is much simpler and remarkable for its naivety. Between the elitism of Plato and the belief that we are all born equal, we have a polarization of attitudes which has become not a question of education but a party political issue. The concept of comprehensive education, whether or not a good thing in itself – and Conservative Leicestershire thought it was a good way of meeting the population explosion – was a popular one because it struck the raw nerve of the 11 + and the inadequacies of post-war education. The translation of the idea of comprehensive education into the reality of split-site schools, neighbourhood schools, migration of staff, inadequate planning, and the absence of proper professional or management training was simply playing with a generation's future. That administrators and teachers achieved as much as they did is remarkable. It has had little effect upon social stratification and the inequalities and inadequacies of the educational system.

The concept of levelling downwards is as unacceptable as promoting privilege. Do we want our doctors to be less well qualified and less numerous? Do we want all our children to be treated the same, irrespective of age, sex, abilities, all wearing the same uniform, eating the same food, for instance? The extremists of egalitarianism would have us believe that all classes should be of mixed ability and that qualifications for university entrance should be removed. They remind one of Groucho Marx's description of American education as 'ages in cages'. Understandably, advocates of the gifted, such as Serebriakoff (1990), argue that 'The influential section of the British public is likely to become less passively tolerant of egalitarian faddism in future. Those who still believe in it may stand and fight if they care to, but it is a lost cause.'

What many advocates of the highly able are advocating, however, is a *meritocracy* in which those who are good at passing tests, have high IQs, who work hard and are conformists, get the right qualifications and run society, with all the self-destructive results envisioned by Michael Young (1958) who coined the word. The apparatchiks and nomenklatura of communism should be warning enough against such an elite. Unfortunately, as we saw when we examined the concept more closely, there is, running through the whole development and application of the concept of intelligence and intelligence testing, a vein of eugenics which, despite the dire warnings of history and the examples of racism in Nazi Germany, South Africa and the USA, still seems to fascinate the gullible.

By politicizing education into extremist camps of egalitarians and elitists, the best interests of children, the best ways of educating them and the best interests of society are ignored. As so often happens, educationists fall into the trap of prescribing for others what they would reject for themselves and denying others what they claim as of right. Plato enjoyed poetry, music and drama but would have proscribed them in his Republic from which the chorybantine revellers would have been banned. While the Warnock Report established the handicapped pupils' right to education according to their needs, it failed to set the goals of that education sufficiently high for them or for the generality of pupils.

Abilities: A Realization of Potential Model

Once, when Charles Dickens made an appeal on behalf of a hospital for sick children, he appealed not on the grounds of the children's suffering, their needs, their helplessness or their innocence, but he appealed to his audience on behalf of the child each one of them had been. What would they have wanted to be done for themselves? The Earl of Chesterfield's dictum, 'Do as you would be done by', has been given a potent twist by John Rawls (1972), who suggests that in making decisions about social policies one should always do so on the basis that the policy-makers might be the most vulnerable and disadvantaged of that society. In other words, this proviso would ensure that policies should include provisions to ensure that no-one is disadvantaged by them. In educational terms, we are arguing for policies in which all children are enabled to realize their potentials, aptitudes, propensities and abilities. This ensures that the best interests of the most and least able are met and that those with special educational or other needs enjoy positive discrimination. To those who are especially anxious that the gifted are provided for, we would ask how we can hope to identify 'the mute inglorious Miltons' unless we first start educating them? Do they assume that we can afford to wait until children are performing their first SATs for assessment at age 7 years or able to do a group IQ test before they hive off the bright ones?

The significance of the concept of realizing human potential is that all children enjoy exposure to all that is worthwhile and life-enhancing in their culture, develop intellectually and in their competencies and, so far as they are able, contribute to that culture and their society. There are many questions such aims raise, some of which we will explore later, in so far as they are relevant to gifted children. It need only be said here that views about what is worthwhile and life-enhancing in our culture may differ and change but it is education which makes us free and that freedom, although not absolute, is the freedom to decide such issues. Deciding how one would be done by in turn leads to the education of those who will ultimately decide how they would be done by. Human progress and survival is dependent upon the transmission of knowledge and experience to successive generations. *La condition humaine* demonstrates how far we have come and how much further we have to travel.

We need to think harder about what we would have wanted for ourselves before deciding the fate of others on such a paltry basis as what will get the most votes or cut the most corners and costs. This is not to ignore the importance of cost-effectiveness and administrative efficiency, but it is to attend to the quality of education delivered, the excellence of its content and the standards achieved by all pupils. This is putting education as a primary source of wealth and at the service of society. When the Warnock Report speaks of education as 'a good thing', it is in this context that we would place it, good in that it serves the best interests of humanity and contributes most to the commonweal. Considerations of this nature are essential if we are to examine the nature of giftedness and make provision for it. Meeting needs is not enough. It is the abilities of our children, whatever their needs, that we must identify and develop. What makes the elitist–egalitarian debate irrelevant is that all children are born as unique individuals, each different from the other, and in developing them and educating them we need to make them more equal by overcoming whatever inabilities they may have and more different from one another by developing their abilities, aptitudes and propensities. From that base we can address the problems of gifted pupils should they have any.

Three Problems

Henry finds school boring. He learnt in primary school not to answer teachers' questions to avoid the sarcasm of his classmates. He alternates between being near the bottom or near the top of his class, giving rise to the comment that he's a dreamer who can do better when he applies himself. Only when he's near the bottom does he find the challenge to catch up. Henry lives for the most part in a private world and it is there that he applies himself to mathematical problems. It is a world of the imagination which he can control with logic and pure reason but at fourteen he has not met anyone with whom to share his world. There are no books in the school library to feed his interest and he uses the public library at weekends as a refuge from the distractions of television at home. None of his teachers is qualified in mathematics and only the Head of Maths would know what Henry was talking about should he discuss his preoccupations. The Head of Maths doesn't know Henry exists.

Karen always does well at school. A pretty, bright girl, eager to please, she finds school a tiresome interruption to her musical and ballet studies. She desperately wants to go to ballet school when she's 17. She is popular with her peers but has little contact with them out of school. Her mother ferries her to her ballet, piano and swimming lessons, her father struggles to pay her fees. What no-one knows is that, behind her ready smile, Karen is secretly worried about her weight. She spends her days at school sitting, PE and games are increasingly rare, and, as she is studying piano and has no singing voice, she has no opportunities to take part in the school's modest musical activities. Karen is 15, apparently successful in school and in her ballet and music. Unfortunately, she is fast becoming anorexic.

Desmond explodes in wild rage if corrected. Most of the time he sits by himself, sunk in despair, scowling, thin and unkempt. He rarely does any written work and never hands in his books to be marked. His teacher respects his grief. Desmond's mother died last month of a brain tumour and his father is dying of cancer. When the class is discussing spring and Easter, Desmond slumps with his head in his hands but, when the class starts to write, Desmond takes out his book and begins writing too. At the end of the lesson he doesn't hand in his book, so, when the class has gone home, the teacher retrieves it from his desk. In it, written in a firm, clear hand with scarcely a correction, are the most vitriolic poems the teacher has ever read. Under the title 'Easter', is a long poem. It begins, 'I spit on you, Christ, with your crown of thorn/ And curse you, God, for letting me be born . . .' Desmond is 10 years old.

It is widely assumed that our education system caters for gifted children. Most LEAs have Advisory Teachers of Gifted Children, educational psychologists are familiar with their problems, the government's Assisted

Places Scheme enables working-class children to attend independent schools appropriate to their gifts and a variety of voluntary bodies, such as the National Association of Gifted Children (NAGC), are able to advise parents. Unfortunately, not all parents or schools are aware of what needs to be done and the concept of giftedness is often limited to academic abilities. As can be seen from the 'problem cases' above, however, we may wonder to what extent an LEA is responsible for the problems experienced by Karen and consider how she might respond were she in a school in which her gifts in music and ballet were nurtured as a normal part of the curriculum. Would Henry's mathematical abilities and general education be improved by private tuition or better staffing? What can be done to help Desmond? What will become of him and his gifts if he is just another case for the Social Services to cope with when his father dies?

We need a clearer understanding of the nature of giftedness and the problems of educating and providing for gifted children and young people, as well as for their families, within both the concept of realizing human potential and the context of the education system.

Whatever Happened to the Gifted Ones?

Interest in gifted children undoubtedly owes a great deal to Lewis N. Terman. In 1906, his PhD was inspired by his interest in Galton and was entitled *Genius and Stupidity*, while his interest in intelligence testing encouraged him to embark on a monumental study of 1528 gifted children selected by a variety of procedures from the 250 000 children in the schools of California. Not only were these children studied in detail, they have been followed up by Terman and his colleagues at Stanford University, and by his successors. The brightest girl had an IQ of over 200, although boys outnumbered girls in the ratio of 115 : 100. The majority were aged 10 and had IQs of 140. Parents and teachers filled out extensive questionnaires about the children's ethnic backgrounds, birth, health and development. They were each given an hour's medical examination and 37 anthropometric measurements were made, together with a 3-hour scholastic achievement battery of tests. Over a third of the cohort was studied in greater detail.

The results showed that the gifted children were not only higher in academic achievements – 44 per cent above the norm – they were fitter, taller, heavier and healthier than on average and were generally superior by every measure whether of personality, traits, interests or social adjustment. This evidence has frequently been quoted to refute the view that gifted children are penalized for their exceptional abilities by poor sensory or physical development or by having personality or other defects.

Follow-up studies of the group have been made at regular intervals (Terman, 1947; Terman and Oden, 1959; Oden, 1968; Janos, 1987). These have shown that the gifted children were usually taller than average and 'probably at least equal or superior to the generality in respect to general health, height, weight, and freedom from serious defects'. As the cohort has aged, the mean IQ has fallen slightly and the most able have moved further ahead of the less able in their career successes, numbers of publications and other measures. Eight times as many of the gifted were in professions than would have been expected and 'both college graduates and nongraduates were filling positions of responsibility and exercising leadership to a reliably greater extent than the generality of college graduates'. Both the men and women earned more than average, were better adjusted both maritally and sexually than average and their children had higher than average IQs.

But, as Professor Steven Ceci of Cornell University reported to the British Psychological Society in April 1991, when the composition of Terman's gifted group is studied, it appears not so surprising that they did so well: 82 per cent of them came from professional and middle-class families. The results are in line with those of Project Talent, a survey of 100 000 children begun in the 1950s which Ceci has also analysed. After social class has been taken into account, IQ bears no relation to success and income in later life. When the cohort members were aged 30, Ceci found no correspondence between IQ and success in terms of income, professional status or other achievements. It is not suggested that Terman consciously distorted his results, rather that his research design was not stringent enough and that it was contaminated by extraneous factors.

A more recent follow-up study of English gifted children growing up is Joan Freeman's (1991) research over 16 years of an original group of 210 children aged 5–14 in 1974–78, which she again surveyed in 1985–88. Of the original group, 170 children and their parents were studied and took part in in-depth interviews in their homes. Freeman took a target sample of 70 children selected from the records of parents who had joined the NAGC. These were matched with two control groups: the first comprised 70 children of the same sex, age, socio-economic background, school class and ability (as measured on the Raven's Progressive Matrices and the revised Stanford-Binet) and the second was matched on all factors save ability. Altogether, 82 of the children had an IQ of 141–70 (the top 1 per cent of the population), 63 were above average with an IQ of 121–40, and 65 were judged average with an IQ of 97–120. Of the sample, 140 were boys and 70 were girls.

This study highlights the individuality of the young people and the dangers of generalizations about gifted children and the provisions for them. Some failed to realize their potential from lack of emotional support and some through poverty. Some tried to act out the stereotype of the misunderstood genius, others felt compelled always to excel; some failed to perform under continuous pressure to do better; some failed to benefit from being accelerated in school; some found social adjustment difficult; some deliberately avoided situations in which they might fail; some were able to adapt successfully and others were given support, a successful education and succeeded. They were all different with different accommodations to experience, different abilities and different needs.

Freeman concludes her study by outlining the lessons to be learned from gifted learners: the need to study how they learn; their need for counselling; the need to match instruction to the child's development; the importance of unstressed early learning at home; the need for teachers to have a wider repertoire of teaching strategies and of appropriate learning strategies for their pupils; the importance of developing creative thinking and creative activities; the need for praise and recognition; the importance of faster learning and for depth and breadth. In schools she rightly stresses the need for flexibility and organization and warns against acceleration unless the child is exceptionally mature. Enrichment, however, should be a natural part of every school; opportunities to meet others of similar abilities and interests at vacation courses are recommended, as is mentoring for gifted children. But Freeman sees the real challenge and opportunity in changing educational policy for all by increased competence and expertise in teaching, by encouraging motivation in learning, thinking and creativity, by parental and adult involvement in the guidance and counselling of pupils and more educational and vocational guidance.

When Professor Benjamin Bloom (1985) and his colleagues at the University of Chicago examined the backgrounds of 25 people successful in music, mathematics, science, sport and art, they found that none had shown outstanding early gifts. What distinguished them was their tenacity and sustained interest over many years. As children, they had not been hot-housed but had been encouraged to have fun and share interests with their parents. Immersion in parental love of music or maths almost from birth was clearly important, but again the absence of pressure and formalized structure was emphasized.

It is the emphasis on the normality of exceptionality which comes through Professor John Radford's (1990) kaleidoscopic survey of the entire field of exceptional early ability. Informed by a mastery of the theoretical and research background of the subject, Radford investigates the topic historically and in almost every aspect of human endeavour. He omits one area, that of medicine, which has always attracted people of high and diverse abilities, but what is surprising is the sweep and scope of

CHAPTER 4

When Learning Explodes

This book is about the happiness and well-being of children as we help them to grow and develop their abilities to their full potential. We put their happiness and well-being first, of course, for humane reasons and because, although it is perfectly possible to develop their abilities without considering these factors, in the short term it will be harder to help, instruct and educate them and, in the long term, they may come to bite or curse the hand that led them, along too difficult and narrow a path, to a lonely and restricted life.

Each child is different and the purpose of education is to make them more individual, more different. Human survival has programmed us that way: not as clones but different so that as a species we may complement and supplement one another. It begins with mating, and the happier that bonding and the longer lasting the bonding is the better for the progeny. Whether or not the happiness and activities of the mother during pregnancy – such as listening to music, reading good books or doing differential calculus – have any effect upon the foetus is debatable, but there is no doubt that her health and avoidance of drink and drugs are vital. What is common to all births is that, however planned or fortuitous they may be, they take place in a social setting. The parents provide the genes, but what combination of them they contribute is a matter of chance. Once born, infants are programmed to elicit in mothers those maternal behaviours, like feeding them, cleaning them, keeping them warm and secure, and singing and talking to them, essential for their survival. In Julian Huxley's words, 'Man added tradition to heredity.'

Mothers are most vulnerable during the infancy of children and need protection and support of the mate and their community. That they often manage almost single-handed is a tribute to their toughness, to hormonal reactions after giving birth and the robustness of babies and their determination to survive come what may. The more help the mother and child have during infancy and the more mutually supportive the roles of father, members of the pair's extended family and the community are, the more rapidly and happily will the child develop. This is particularly true in our complex and diverse culture.

The infant is not a passive recipient but an active participant in the survival game. Infants are curious and demanding in their zest for survival and they learn fast. Some learn so fast that, before they can walk or talk, they have trained their parents to respond to their every demand. They may become the children with the drone syndrome who don't learn to read because they've trained their parents to carry on reading to them long after there was any reason why they should, and of whom, when they run into trouble, their parents say, 'But we've always given them everything they wanted.' On the other hand, parents who fail to interact appropriately with their infants, because, for example, they are stressed and distracted, may well induce *mal de mere*, sickness with mother, in their offspring.

The learning in a social setting which takes place between mother and child in the first 3 years is of vital formative and developmental significance. The plasticity and receptiveness of the questing brain of infants even enables some to surmount perinatal insults and to acquire the language of their culture and manipulate its rhythms, its sounds and its grammatical rules whether that language be Japanese, Urdu or English. This alone demonstrates the enormous learning capacity of infants, yet, in the first years of life, they also learn to be mobile, dexterous, become socialized and remarkably skilful. It is not surprising, therefore, that given encouragement and the right environmental conditions, some children learn so much more.

It is in these early years that they are learning attitudes and values. Some are learning to be amused, stuck for hours before a television set. Some are beginning to learn the language of music or mathematics. Some are learning the rewards of curiosity, while others learn not to ask too many questions. Nor should we be surprised if, lacking encouragement and the right environment, some children learn so little. A hungry child wants to be fed and is an incurious child. The National Children's Home survey found that none of the 354 families with children under 5 years on income support was eating a healthy diet. The brain, when we are active or at rest, demands a steady supply of protein. Yet, some children, despite being born into the most disadvantaging conditions of an impoverished environment, survive to make unique contributions to society. Lewis Latimer, son of a fugitive slave, drew up the plans for Bell's telephone and perfected the filament for his electric light.

The most creative act we can perform as a species is to bring up children to become socially adjusted, cultured and life-enhancing adults able to contribute to their culture. It is the least appreciated and least understood of our creative abilities. Even parents who are geniuses can get it wrong. J.S. Bach wanted his son Immanuel to become a lawyer, no doubt for the best of practical reasons, and only just in time recognized that Immanuel would never realize himself if he was not allowed to pursue his gifts as a musician. John Stuart Mill and Norbert Weiner received rigorous education in childhood which undoubtedly contributed to their brilliance, but both complained that it had seriously warped their personalities. Before we start hot-housing children we need to consider their vulnerability and their social and emotional needs and recognize that without wide social and cultural experience, the willing child of today may have grave difficulties in coping with the biological explosion of adolescence or the responsibilities and role of the adult world.

Learning to use language is much more than establishing a communications system. Understanding what is happening in infancy is the key to understanding the future development of children in our culture and the ways in which some children may become gifted. Bruner (1983) sums up the position when he sets forth

> . . . a view of language acquisition that makes it continuous with and dependent on the child's acquisition of his culture. Culture is constituted of symbolic procedures, concepts, and distinctions that can only be made in language. It is constituted for the child in the very act of mastering language. Language, in consequence, cannot be understood save in its cultural setting.

The study of this process has been illuminated by Kaye (1982) in his *The Mental and Social Life of Babies: How Parents Create Persons*. He points out that a child inherits biologically and, to a large extent, also inherits his or her environment and culture. Any infant can learn any language, and not only do we inherit an ability to learn: 'Along with learning ability, the human species evolved teaching ability.' It is through the interaction of learning child with teaching parent, which begins at birth, that the infant gradually becomes a person.

This shared system, in which the infant is likened by Kaye to an apprentice who 'learns the trade because the master provides protected opportunities to practice selected sub-tasks, monitors the growth of apprentice's skills and gradually presents more difficult tasks', operates because there is shared meaning and purpose through joint doing. The adult provides frames of behaviour which structure the child's world. Some of the most common frames Kaye describes are: the *nutrient frame* in which the child is nourished, comforted, cleansed, consoled and fondled; the *protective frame* which keeps the child within earshot, away from dangers such as fire or water; the *instrumental frame* in which the adult anticipates the child's intention as when she moves a toy within the infant's reach; the *feedback frame* in which the parent's praise or admonitory warning 'No!' instructs and shapes behaviour; the *modelling frame* in which the adult performs an action and waits for the infant to imitate it – an example of turn-taking which is a key activity in early learning; the *discourse frame* which may start with a tickle to elicit a laugh and extend to song or riddle; and the *memory frame* in which the adult uses knowledge of shared experiences to organize new experiences. As most parents know, most of these *frames* may be enjoyed as *games*.

The apprenticeship model is a good one which is relevant not only to the first months of infancy and throughout the child's acquisition of language but one, according to Kaye, which we see 'in successively more sophisticated systems as one of the invariant functions of human development, extrinsic to the child but nonetheless a birthright of the species'. Understanding it helps us to understand the ways in which some children become exceptionally able. The parent knows the language and leads the child by a variety of strategies to play the language game. Some parents know the language of music or mathematics and their children learn to play those games with them, too.

The complexities of the process by which children learn language need not concern us here. Suffice it to say that children learn partly by imitation, partly by experimentation – as when they babble to themselves, and largely by interaction with their parents. By 12 months they may have said their first words and show signs of understanding instructions, and then, suddenly, their vocabulary seems to explode. It is not surprising that Chomsky (1968) characterized this innate facility in gaining language as a Language Acquisition Device (LAD). Bruner emphasizes the parents' role as the Language Acquisition Support System (LASS). In real-life situations of their shared experiences in which the meaning is clear to the child, language is bounced back and forth and the language game is played with growing complexity, the parent acting as the child's language bank. Professor Barbara Tizard and M. Hughes (1984) studied tape-recordings of busy parents going about their everyday activities at home and found that they were averaging 27 conversations with their pre-school children in an hour. A year later, she found that the same children in nursery school were only averaging 10 conversational exchanges every hour with their teachers.

The language-rich environment of the home, especially when it is enriched by other children and the extended family and/or actively involved friends, is the ideal setting for both the language and the cognitive development of children. Unfortunately, concerned and capable parents have been inhibited from exploiting the opportunities for extending this interaction beyond the pre-school years. When working with gifted, cerebral palsied children and 'dyslexic' pupils, we found that the children's greatest progress was made when their parents could be encouraged to take an active part in their education. When they are both encouraged to do so and assured that the ways in which they helped their children to learn to use and understand language, to walk and do so many things were the best ways, they are at first incredulous, on reflection reassured and, as soon as they start teaching their children, delighted with the rapidity with which they see results. Before elaborating upon this instructional model, it is instructive to look at what most parents teach their children in the first 5 pre-school years. In importance, quality and quantity, the achievements demonstrate the power of the model and the ability of parents to teach and of children to learn.

Achievements of Parental Instruction in the First 5 Years

- Full mobility including jumping and climbing.
- Feeding using cutlery.
- Dressing, including tying knots, using buttons and zips.
- Toilet training.
- Washing.
- Uses and understands language with vocabulary of 2000 + words and correct grammatical structures; able to follow and give instructions; define things by their use; describe, compare and contrast; uses language appropriate to social relationships and to guide actions; follows and tells stories; argues and reasons (egotistically); asks and answers questions.
- Enjoys jokes, sees incongruities and has sense of humour.
- Skips, hops, skates, kicks and catches balls, cycles.
- Plays alone, with others, takes turns and follows simple game rules.
- Knows own name, sex, age, birth date, address and way round neighbourhood.
- Uses pencils, crayons, brushes to draw people, houses, common objects; circles, squares, lines, triangles (not a diamond).
- Counts to *c.* 20, knows fingers on each hand, recognizes digits, repeats numbers such as 75364.
- Cuts out common shapes with scissors, models in 3D.

- Enjoys being read to and reading or has begun to read and recognizes some words and letters.
- Writes own name and most letters of alphabet – some are able to write messages or enjoy copying.
- With supervision able to care for younger sibling, pets and perform useful chores around home.

Many children will have achieved even more than this depending on their circumstances. There is ample evidence in the lives of many gifted people that their abilities were first developed and formed in these early years. Some may already swim, have read many books, dance, knit or be bi- or tri-lingual and, in poor communities, may be working. Some perfectly normal children may still have many of these benchmarks to achieve and variations between members of the same family are considerable.

It should not surprise us, however, if some children by the age of 5 have learned other skills in mathematics or music. Jacqueline du Pré could climb when she was 4 years old:

> I remember being in the kitchen at home, looking up at the old-fashioned wireless. I climbed onto the ironing board, switched it on, and heard an introduction to the instruments of the orchestra . . . It didn't make much of an impression on me until they got to the cello, and then . . . I fell in love with it straightaway. Something within the instrument spoke to me, and it's been my friend ever since.

She told her mother that she wanted 'to make that sound'. She began learning, standing up, with a full-size cello. Her mother, herself a trained musician, had known Jackie was musical from an early age, singing tunes at 18 months and, when she was 4 years old, picking out tunes on the piano which she had heard her older and talented sister, Hilary, play. The Russian pianist Andrei Gavrilov tells how exasperating he must have been when, aged 3, he corrected his 6-year-old brother's playing of Tchaikovsky. His brother took up painting.

When Mrs du Pré tapped on her 18-month-old daughter's high chair and Jacqueline tapped out the same rhythm, they were demonstrating the significance of shared meaning. Kaye (1982) emphasizes the importance of this in the cognitive development of children: 'Only where there is shared meaning can there be shared purpose. So shared meaning is essential to the definition of a social system.' This is the essential building block of all learning and of the immersion of children in their culture with its gestures, signs and symbols. As children assimilate experience and understanding of their world in situations such as that, they also gain models of imitation. Moreover, the parents lead development, initiate activities just beyond the child's abilities. They know the child wants to ride a bike and that she can't do so. Educationists in analogous situations may say the child should wait until she can and meanwhile do a project about wheels. The parent sits the child on the bike, supports the child and praises her for steering. Soon the child is not just imitating riding, she is riding. The parent reads to the child, plays the game of getting her to guess what comes next and one day she's reading. Imitation is a valid and often underestimated way of learning. 'Example,' as Dr Johnson acknow-ledged, 'is always more efficacious than precept'. Opportunities for trying skills with someone we trust and who provides a model of execution enable us to gain competency much more quickly than if we are left to puzzle out how to perform them alone. They break skills down to help us build them up. All these activities in which parents traditionally involve their children are not conscious attempts to teach assimilation, represen-tation, signification and symbols, but play for the fun of it, showing off, pretending, having a good time and, also, ways of succeeding and achieving.

Kaye says that what mothers do in different ways is make their babies into persons and themselves into their best friends. In the acquisition of language, 'In a sense, the mother is not really talking to the baby. She is talking *for* the baby, to herself.' By learning language in this interacting, socializing way, children learn to internalize, to recall and relate and to think. There are no limits to the range of activities we may teach our children in these early years if we wish, but there are limits to what we should attempt to teach them.

Children assume that what we teach them is important for their sur-vival and if we think it a good thing it is a good thing. The 4-year-olds taken to the ice-rink in the hope that one day they will become stars have lots of falls, knocks and bruises and 20 years of hard work ahead of them if they are to achieve even modest success. It is widely held that 5 is considered the optimum age at which children should start to learn a stringed instrument. John Stuart Mill was taught Greek at the age of 3. Tennis champions go on getting younger. Shirley Temple danced and sang her way to be the youngest Oscar winner aged 6. While most chil-dren are beginning to learn to read some are already using computer languages. What we must ask ourselves is how worthwhile are the skills we want our children to learn and what measures will be taken to ensure the children's all-round development. In 1801, Pestalozzi summed up the position thus:

> All human instruction is no more than the art of helping nature in its forceful search to develop in its own way, and this art depends primarily on the relation and harmony between the impressions to be made upon the child and the specific stage which his developing powers have reached at the time.

se infants trust their parents, they are in no position to decide independently what is in their best long-term interests. By and large, society applauds children's success in academic and artistic fields and it is charmed to read stories about Yehudi Menuhin deciding at 4 that he wanted to learn the violin and 3 years later performing Mendelssohn's Violin Concerto with maturity. The public is less likely to applaud prodigies who have been trained to gamble at poker, but there are many grey areas and, for the best of reasons, the law protects children from exploitation on the stage. It is easier, too, to applaud prodigies if we believe they are possessed of some gift which they have been fortunate or favoured enough to develop than if we believe that there are no such things as gifts and that they were ordinary kids whose parents accelerated their development by some form of hot-housing.

Nature or Nurture?

The truth of the matter lies between these two extremes. We need what the Russian educator Makarenko (1954) called 'a sense of the mean'. Howe (1990a) argues that 'no child ever inherited a special gift, or an innate talent, or a natural ability', but attributes exceptional abilities to the early differences between infants. These differences, 'some of which are probably inborn and possibly inherited, that can have effects of various kinds on later development form just one of a large number of interacting factors that, together, help to determine the child's future capabilities'. There is a circularity here: no child inherits a special gift but some children are different from others and become exceptionally able. If we apply Occam's Razor and define giftedness as exceptional ability, we can prevent entities such as reification, eugenics, genetic predestination and circularity being produced beyond necessity.

Although Howe (1990b) maintains that, 'Research investigators have failed to discover any inherited or genetic traits that correspond to the popular notion of a natural gift or talent', at the most basic level it is possible to identify inherited physical characteristics which enable some children to become athletes in specific activities, such as gymnastics and jumping, and which prevent others from even attempting them. Again, it is possible to identify children with an innate sense of rhythm which may be of advantage to them in acquiring a variety of skills from dancing and touch-typing to music and verse-making, and others born with two left feet who never know their left hand from their right and who could never hope to become professional dancers.

While no-one would argue that possessing absolute or perfect pitch is essential for anyone wishing to be a musician, it is certainly an ability or gift which Mozart, MacDowell, Menuhin and many other musicians had, which some developed but Schumann and Wagner and many others did not have. Moreover, having absolute pitch can, in certain circumstances, be a disadvantage to musicians. But it *is* an ability of musical significance. Dr Joseph Profita and his colleagues at the University of California, after studying 400 subjects from 60 families whose members have absolute pitch, are currently attempting to identify the gene on the chromosome which determines it. When Howe argues that no-one is born with all the attributes of musicianship or mathematical ability, he is no doubt quite right. But when, in everyday usage, we observe the natural way in which some children acquire skills and say they are gifted, we are only expressing in one word what he is explaining in many. The value of what he says lies in the importance he places upon observing children closely, as they develop and change, in order to identify their uniqueness and, in Pestalozzi's words, in harmony with the child, helping nature in its forceful search to develop in its own way.

The danger of putting undue emphasis on the importance of nurture is that we may interpret this as meaning that we can make any child into a world-class musician, sumo wrestler, ballet dancer or mathematician. We know that we can educate all children, but it would be folly to imagine that they can all aspire to the same high levels of performance in all fields of human endeavour. That road leads to force-feeding and cruelty. We can learn from the crises which Mill, Ruskin, Weiner, Jacqueline du Pré and Judy Garland suffered to ensure that, in educating our children, we try to prepare them for adolescence and the adult world. Imposing our wills or ambitions upon vulnerable children who need to play and enjoy the company of their peers is to add to their vulnerability. Whatever parts heredity or chance may play, growing up in a loving, caring, culturally rich, stimulating, involving, demanding and rewarding environment is the best possible start children can have.

Parents recognize their children's differences and are sensitive to them. Often they see attributes, characteristics and defects others, including professionals, fail to discern. Most medical specialists and teachers have today abandoned their old-world airs of omniscience and listen carefully to what parents can tell them about their children. But often we underestimate children, in and out of school, and parents are reinforced in this when they are given the impression that they should surrender their children to professional educators and not interfere. Even when a child shows interest and abilities in which the parent is completely incompetent, the parent should both attempt to take an active interest in the child's progress and endeavour to develop all the other aspects of the child's abilities and interests. Not all parents of exceptionally able children are themselves outstanding in any particular field, and this may be a distinct advantage in helping children to grow up with a much broader and deeper perspective of life.

If we wish our children to develop their abilities in infancy we need to make their cultural interaction with us as rich and enjoyable as possible and, at the same time, sharpen their focus of attention upon whatever they are engaged in with us. Mathematics is a language and, if we wish, we can focus attention upon its vocabulary and structure by developing the common games we play. Providing it is all a game in which the child always wins approval, progress will be rapid. We commonly count as we hold their hands and ascend a flight of stairs. We can encourage them to count with us. Descending stairs we can count backwards. We count their fingers and toes. We can count in fives. We count their ears, hands, eyes, knees, elbows and feet and we can count them in twos. In this way, sets and patterns of numbers are introduced from the earliest days. Cutting things up for them and naming two halves, four quarters and eight eighths introduces fractions. The mathematically aware parent will see many opportunities for introducing prime, square and cube numbers and identifying the geometric shapes in the child's three-dimensional world.

Human knowledge grows by being particular. We start by discriminating between shrubs and trees, between coniferous and deciduous trees and end up studying parasites on fungi on a variety of pine in the tundra. Particularizing may mean no more than distinguishing between iris, eyebrow, pupil and eyelid, between moths and butterflies, between door, cill, architrave and hinge, so that many times a day the child enjoys renewal of Helen Keller's discovery that, 'Everything had a name, and each name gave birth to a new thought.'

We will encourage, too, memory of what has been introduced. Bright children are usually children who remember things, often with little apparent conscious effort. The absent-minded professor may forget her husband's birthday but lecture without notes. One of the most underestimated abilities of children is their ability to retain and recall, but too often this faculty is not exercised because so few demands are made upon the cycle of regarding, recording, retaining, rehearsing and recalling. If we begin by assuming children remember and expect them to, they will quickly learn to do so. If we prompt them when necessary and reward their recollection they will soon remember with little conscious effort. Of course, parents and teachers are always being warned about the dangers of rote learning but, unfortunately, are rarely told what should replace it. The objection to rote learning is not to the repetition but to learning without understanding. Even this is a doubtful objection, but what we want to encourage is efficient memorization of what is understood and is meaningful and·significant. Repetition is something children love. They enjoy exercising skills and don't mind not succeeding first time. Watch them with computer games or trying to stand on their heads, do cartwheels, skip or catch a ball.

Repetition is practice and practice is persistence. Young children are often impatient and impetuous. They see something and immediately reach out for it. If they can't reach it, they howl. As part of helping them to grow up parents wean them away from these behaviours. What we want to encourage is purposeful practice of skills. This is essential for musicians, artists and scientists. No matter how great their aptitudes or ambitions, they cannot hope to realize their potential without practice. Skills have to become automatized. The autonomic system is in-built, and therefore we don't have to practise breathing but we do have to practise skills like playing an instrument, doing high jumps or entrechats. Practice that is purposeful is enjoyable if it is appropriate to our level of competency and we can see point and purpose in it. But, with children, practice must be built up slowly and systematically. In learning to memorize and to practise, they are learning something which is absolutely essential for the vast majority of us. They are learning application and dedication.

Parental attitudes are the hidden curriculum which infants absorb with their milk. If we are caring and reflective, so will our children be. For the most part, noisy parents have noisy children, quiet parents have quiet children. It is vitally important to encourage children to be curious and enquiring. Most of them are born that way, but too many learn not to be. If parents are seen to be questioning, curious and enquiring, then the chances are that the children will be. Children are often reprimanded by stressed and tired parents for asking 'Why? Why?' What should be discouraged are mindless questions for the purpose of attention seeking. Treating children's questions seriously is, of course, important, but often throwing the questions back at them with a friendly, 'Well, what do you think?', or another question which will lead them to think out the answers for themselves, are useful strategies. The simple, direct answer is all that they most often want, but there is no reason why the children's questions should not sometimes lead to a discussion. Questions provide valuable clues to what is going on in children's minds and thus provide opportunities for parents to help them develop, extend or apply their thinking.

In all of these activities, what we are also encouraging is learning set. The more children learn about the real world the more they learn about how to think. Learning to learn is being developed in these early years.

Zones of Proximal Development

The 7-year-olds were all fairly familiar with notation of thousands, hundreds, tens and units and their teacher wondered whether they were ready to grapple with decimals. Quickly, she revised place values. She wrote 1 111 on the board. She put in the decimal point and a one after it: 1 111.1. 'So, if I go down, hundreds, tens, units – what does this one stand for?' she asked, pointing at the .1. There were many blank faces but a dozen hands were eagerly raised. 'A tenth', one girl burst out. 'Yes, but what about this one?' the teacher asked, putting another one after the tenth, .11. Ten hands were raised this time. 'A hundredth?' ventured a boy, tentatively. 'Right. So what about this one?' asked the teacher adding another digit. Only five hands were raised. 'A thousandth!' the girl exploded.

Although all the children were competent at the level of understanding place value in whole numbers, only a few understood decimal fractions. None had been taught this, but the teacher's prompting, by drawing attention to the descending order of magnitude, was enough to enable some of them to infer the decimal place values. The teacher's strategy is a common one, used in a variety of circumstances and in all subjects. It is a way of keeping interest and attention alive, a way of checking that pupils fully understand, and a way of enabling the more able pupils to exercise their problem-solving abilities. It is a technique, too, used in Piagetian tests of cognition, but it was Vygotsky who saw its significance as a diagnostic instrument. Luria (1972), the Russian neuropsychologist, has said of him:

> Vygotsky was a genius. After more that half a century in science I am unable to name another person who even approaches his incredible analytic ability and foresight. All of my work has been no more than the working out of the psychological theory which he constructed.

Vygotsky (1962) describes how, in the 1930s (he died in 1934 aged only 38), he realized that two children aged 10 years with the same backgrounds and apparent development ages of 8 years, as determined by standardized tests could, in fact, perform differently. When he helped them solve problems, one child could perform at a level 3 years in advance of the other: one 10 year-old performing at the 9-year-old level, the other at the 12-year-old level. The difference between their performance and developmental ages, between 8 and 9 and between 8 and 12, he termed the zone of proximal development. 'Experience has shown that the child with the larger zone of proximal development will do much better at school. This measure gives a more helpful clue than mental age does to the dynamics of intellectual progress.' The term is sometimes translated as 'the zone of potential development'. Vygotsky (1962) defines the zone as:

The zone of proximal development is the distance between the actual developmental level as determined by independent problem solving and the level of potential development as determined through problem solving under adult guidance or in collaboration with more able peers . . . It defines those functions that have not yet matured but are in the process of maturation, functions that will mature tomorrow but are currently in an embryonic state . . . The actual developmental level characterizes mental development retrospectively, while the zone of proximal development characterizes mental development prospectively . . . Thus, the zone of proximal development permits us to delineate the child's immediate future and his dynamic developmental state, allowing not only for what already has been achieved developmentally but also for what is in the course of maturing . . . The state of a child's mental development can be determined only by clarifying its two levels: the actual developmental level and the zone of proximal development.

Vygotsky goes on to discuss the significance of this concept in the context of learning and points out that *'learning which is oriented toward developmental levels that have already been reached is ineffective from the viewpoint of a child's overall development. It does not aim for a new stage of the developmental process but rather lags behind this process. Thus, the notion of a zone of proximal development enables us to propound a new formula, namely, that the only "good learning" is that which is in advance of development.'*

There are two major implications to be drawn from this concept so far as gifted pupils are concerned:

1. In identifying gifted pupils we need to assess not merely the levels at which they are functioning but their zone of proximal development; in other words, how far they are able to progress with some instruction.
2. In educating gifted pupils, as with all pupils, the only good education is that which leads to their development.

Together, these concepts of development and instruction underline the importance of identifying gifted pupils and the stultifying effects of failing to develop their potential. Vygotsky saw, too, that in play and imaginative and creative situations, a zone of proximal development is formed in which:

. . . a child behaves above his average age, above his daily behaviour; in play it is as though he were a head taller than himself . . . From the point of view of development, creating an imaginary situation can be regarded as a means of developing abstract thought.

Once we recognize the significance and value of children's experience beyond school, their everyday, 'spontaneous' experiences and learning, we can provide the structures which transform them into the scientific and systematized knowledge, the tools of thought which are the power amplifiers of our culture. The emphasis which Vygotsky placed upon the role of teaching in the development of thought is underlined by his recognition that, whilst concept formation begins in earliest childhood, intellectual functions ripen, take shape and develop only at puberty: 'If the environment presents no such tasks to the adolescent, makes no new demands on him, and does not stimulate his intellect by providing a sequence of new goals, his thinking fails to reach the highest stages, or reaches them with great delay.' Throughout his studies of the education process, Vygotsky emphasizes the importance of making spontaneous learning conscious:

> The child has a command of the grammar of his native tongue long before he enters school, but it is unconscious, acquired in a purely structural way . . . our analysis clearly showed the study of grammar to be of paramount importance for the mental development of the child. Grammar and writing help the child to rise to a higher level of speech development.

He recognized, too, that instruction in a given subject influences the development of higher functions far beyond the confines of that subject; that consciousness and deliberate mastery were common to all subjects and the main contribution of the school years: 'It follows from these findings that all the basic school subjects act as formal discipline, each facilitating the learning of the others; the psychological functions stimulated by them develop in one complex process.' In view of this, Vygotsky was concerned that, if instruction should march ahead of development and lead it, and be aimed not so much at the ripe as the ripening functions,

> It remains necessary to determine the lowest threshold at which instruction in, say, arithmetic may begin . . . For each subject of instruction there is a period when its influence is most fruitful because the child is most receptive to it. It has been called the *sensitive period* by Montessori and other educators . . . Our investigations demonstrated the social and cultural nature of the development of the higher functions during these periods, i.e. its dependence on co-operation with adults and on instruction.

Our understanding of the role parents play in the education of their children in the development of thought and language gives new significance to Vygotsky and his emphasis on determining the earliest time at which instruction may begin, the critical learning periods, or what Bruner refers to as 'readiness to learn'. In his brilliant study of the mental and social life of babies, Kaye (1982) has written what he acknowledges 'can be regarded as an extension of Vygotsky's ideas down to the years before language. I have argued that parents, in making the child a member of their preexisting system, induce the development of mind.'

If we agree with Vygotsky and Kaye that 'communication is the origin of mind', we can see how vital are the early years of infancy for the development of abilities and characteristics, whether these be cognitive or orectic. We can see this clearly when children develop so rapidly in the social environment of the family in 'languages' such as music and mathematics. Prokoviev not only learned to play the piano brilliantly but, before he was 12, had written two operas. Mozart performed in public aged 5, Mendelssohn aged 9. Gauss was correcting his father's sums when only 3 years old. Ampère had mastered advanced mathematics by 12. It is this early development of children with remarkable propensities which makes it so difficult to decide how many of their abilities are inherited and how many the result of nurture. We would be unwise to underestimate the importance of the latter.

CHAPTER 5

Learning to
Learn to be Gifted

Learning to learn is learning to think and to apply what has been learned to appropriate situations. Without learning skills, whether physical or intellectual, no matter what potential children may have, there can be no abilities. We can develop or inhibit learning and we can shape it in ways appropriate to our culture. Infants on the Solomon Islands are kept from under trees, because of the danger of falling coconuts, and kept away from the sea. Eskimo children learn to name the many kinds of ice in their environment. Many children come to school already reading, others come to school regarding reading as an almost alien activity. Sex-typing and class-typing affect attitudes to learning because they limit the range of activities esteemed by children. If we want our children to increase their knowledge and skills, we should avoid typing of this sort and encourage open-mindedness. Anti-intellectualism and inverted snobbery are common in our society. Manual abilities are poorly paid or indulged as hobbies and therapies. In the 1980s, aggression and confrontation were given greater regard than consensus and cooperation. These all have a bearing on values and, thus, on what is taught and learned.

As children develop, they have to learn that there are constraints upon what they may do, upon how they may behave in specific circumstances and upon how they may think. This, too, is part of their cultural/social heritage. For example, we want them at both the moral and scientific levels to have regard for the truth, for reason and logic. Similarly, we want them to explore their universe but to avoid poisoning or injuring themselves or others. The apprenticeship model we explored in the previous Chapter still holds good. Bruner (1983) writes:

One sets the game, provides a scaffold to assure that the child's ineptitudes can be rescued by appropriate intervention, and then removes the scaffold part by part as the reciprocal structure can stand on its own.

Learning is the progressive reduction of uncertainty and, in the words of Vygotsky, instruction leads development. It is in this respect that, as we have seen, Kaye describes his own work as an extension of Vygotsky's theories and, in particular, of his concept that 'communication is the origin of mind'.

Parents and teachers who awaken interest and attention, structure and support their children's acquisition of skills and knowledge, give feedback and knowledge of results and reward their efforts with praise, are developing the parent–child interactive model and teaching them to learn to learn and, ultimately, to think for themselves. A considerable literature has grown up analysing the components of this structuring and scaffolding (Rogoff and Lave, 1984) and, following Vygotsky and Bruner, the development of cognitive abilities in children.

Goal-directed Learning: Pieces of String

The concept we have evolved to help parents and teachers reflects that research. It is an interactive instructional model of developing and involving all aspects of the child in the realization of successive goals towards mastery. This can be summed up in the mnemonic PIECES of STRING: the Physical, Intellectual, Emotional, Cultural, Educational and Social dimensions of the child being directed towards the realization of Short-Term Realizable INteresting Goals. The power of this model lies in the importance it places upon, so far as is possible or appropriate, involving the whole of the child's persona, of indicating alternative routes to learning (e.g. giving a child a physical, concrete experience of an abstract idea or concept), and in its recognition that we ignore any of these dimensions at the child's peril. The model is also readily capable of extension. It suggests its obvious omissions. The Physical dimension includes the sensory, the Emotional includes the motivational, the Intellectual includes factors such as curiosity and problem solving, the concept of Goals suggests TOTE (Test–Operate–Test–Exit) units of learning, the Realizable reminds us of the importance, too, of Realistic and Relevant goals, INteresting reminds us of the importance of tasks being intrinsically and extrinsically appropriate to the child's level of development.

Exceptionally able children may demonstrate their abilities not only in their rapid comprehension and mastery of the successive steps we put before them and in their extended zone of proximal development, but also by their strong drive to succeed. They are often strongly self-motivated and happily take off on their own. Here the parent or teacher may need to moderate this strong self-drive for a variety of reasons. It is increasingly important in our diverse culture that, while advancing on a narrow front, say in prodding the computer or playing the flute, the broader aspects of social life – playing with one's peers, reading widely, being familiar with the arts and sciences – are also enjoyed. This is not always as easy as we might wish. Children and young people find security in being single-minded. Task absorption in one activity can become task avoidance of other fields. Great skill and tact may be necessary in encouraging these broader interests as opposed to imposing them. If imposed they will be regarded as boring and unnecessary distractions.

We must remember, too, that we need to keep the options open for children. The physicist of today may be the architect of the future, the horse-rider of today may be the opera singer of tomorrow. Manuel de Falla decided on his true vocation when he was 8 years old. He would be a writer and entered a fantasy life from which he had no wish to be distracted. It was hearing Haydn's *Stabat Mater* which changed his mind and started him upon his career as a composer. And Haydn? Born in a poor wheelwright's cottage in Croatia, he was surrounded by folk music and attended the local choir school when 6 years old before going as a chorister to St Stephen's Cathedral, Vienna, aged 8. The tunes and rhythms of folk music enliven Haydn's compositions.

Models for Performance

If we know where we wish to lead children and can break down the successive steps to that goal, we will want to be sure that each step is mastered and the importance of practice and revision will be incorporated into our instruction. Gifted children may be impatient to move on and we need to create opportunities for them to concentrate on aspects of their performance which they may too readily wish to hurry past. The fluent reader may be a poor calligrapher and a slipshod speller in her anxiety to put down her fleeting thoughts. We can make an opportunity for her to slow down by suggesting she rewrites whatever she has written for someone special to read. Young musicians who must prepare for competitions, performances and their grade examinations are, thereby, given purpose for practice and attention to the details and niceties they might otherwise ignore. Young athletes and games players are given similar purpose in the practice of their skills by the meetings, matches and events in which they take part. Giving purpose by a sense of special occasion is often the best way of encouraging purposeful practice and attention to detail.

Here, too, our own behaviours as parents or teachers are important. Children are acute observers of adults and their foibles. They are also, around the age of 7, acutely aware of fairness and consistency. Few of us would claim to be models of perfection, but we can attempt at least to practise what we preach to them.

But there may come a time when children's progress and demands outstrip parents' abilities, energies or available time. Gifted children also need to be with other children, with some of whom they can share their interests and with others whose abilities and interests are very different from their own. In the vast majority of cases, other things being equal, parents are the ideal teachers and models for the first 3 years. In some cases, grandparents or relatives including older siblings, may fill the interactive role for many of the children's waking hours. What about nurseries? Are there criteria on which they may be judged and what part can they play in the realization of children's – particularly gifted children's – potential?

The Role of Nurseries

Apart from providing for the basic needs of children in terms of shelter, warmth, security and food, child-minders, crèches and day nurseries cannot be expected to provide adequately for the emotional, social and intellectual needs of young children. At best they can only be regarded as a last resort and it is one of the tragedies of the increased numbers of single-parent families and the thousands of families living in poverty that it is so often the children whose needs are the greatest who are most badly provided for.

The good nursery school, however, in which the children's education is considered of paramount importance, may well provide for the generality of children and the children of high ability. In the USA, nursery education provision designed to develop children's cognitive skills, under the Headstart programme for disadvantaged children, has been evaluated as so successful that, according to Professor Weikart (Weikart *et al.*, 1978a, b; see also Weber *et al.*, 1978), every dollar spent on it represents a saving of $6 which would have been needed to have been spent later on social and educational interventions.

Parents who send children to nursery schools expect their children to receive educational and social advantages which they would not otherwise have if they stayed at home. They want, too, to feel that they are included in, not excluded from, what goes on in the school. It has been said that, when kindergartens were first set up, middle-class parents patronized them so that their children could do all the things, like making a noise and a mess, they weren't allowed to do at home. There is still confusion in many people's minds about what is disparagingly called 'The Play Way, which involves merry teachers having jolly fun in disorderly classes of romping, playful children' (Serebriakoff, 1990). In fact, the tradition of nursery education is founded upon the ideas of Pestalozzi, Froebel, Montessori and, in this country, Margaret MacMillan and Susan and Nathan Isaacs, which were rooted in a concern for the social and cognitive development of children. As we discuss in Chapter 6, the concept of play needs careful study and cannot be dismissed so lightly, but parents certainly don't want their children to go to nursery school to waste their time in unsupervised and undirected play. They may certainly want structured learning through play.

So far as the best interest of the children is concerned, parents need to look realistically at what they can provide in the pre-school years and what nursery education may be able to provide. Many parents feel more secure if they know that their children are receiving education by professionals but a growing number of parents, some 10 000 of them, favour home education. A solution which is particularly appropriate for gifted children is part-time nursery education. If the nursery school offers a wide range of stimulating activities at a high level, it may well provide a broader educational and social experience for the bright child. It is often argued that family and neighbourhood friends provide the social experience children need with their peers and with children older and younger than themselves as well as with adults who are not family or family friends. Sometimes this may be so, but in the majority of cases children benefit from this exposure to a wider community than the often claustrophobic atmosphere of the family. The nursery school as a controlled learning environment may well be a bridge to the community and a robust preparation for school.

Ideally, what parents want from nursery schools is a continuation of the social and intellectual education which they have begun. What they will look for, therefore, is set out below.

Criteria for Nursery School Education

- Lively, qualified and experienced head, with good management skills and personal relations.
- Governing/management body on which parents are represented.
- Clear objectives set out simply and in writing, without jargon, of what the school aims to achieve for all its pupils in terms of specific educational, cultural and social goals.

- Daily programme of activities.
- Good staffing ratio of qualified teachers of 1:12 maximum.
- Additional nursery assistants: a minimum of one per group.
- Rota of parental attendance.
- Curricula for language oral development, reading, writing, science, mathematics, drama, music, physical education and art.
- Programme of local visits and of visitors to school.
- Attractive surroundings, interior and exterior, free of hazards and litter.
- Outside play activity/games area with part covered space and part children's garden.
- Pets and/or living, growing things.
- Child-scale toilet and cloakroom facilities.
- Child-size tables and chairs, work-benches, sinks, display and storage facilities.
- Plentiful and attractively displayed books, resources for all subjects including maths, music, science, art, PE, etc.
- Displays of stimulus materials in good variety and of high quality.
- Displays of children's written work, models, art, problem-solving activities, etc.
- Facilities for group and solo study.
- Working atmosphere of purposeful buzz with strong task orientation.
- Good teacher–child and child–child dialogue: children speaking out clearly and confidently.
- Complete absence of bullying.
- All children with clear idea of what they are doing and why they are doing it.
- Where meals are provided, a varied and nutritious diet.
- First-aid and sick-bay facilities.

In Place of Hot-housing

The good nursery school may well be the ideal solution but, in terms of nursery provision, England comes almost at the bottom of the European league table, only above Portugal. The inspired work being done to help parents develop children's cognitive skills, from the early months through to 5 years, on the Pilton housing estate, Edinburgh, is financed in Holland. If we are concerned to realize the potential of all our children and ensure that, in particular, their development in their pre-school years is as full as possible, we must first ensure that all social inequalities adversely affecting them are removed. Poor housing, poor diet, poor parenting by parents locked in the poverty trap without hope of escape, poor experience and lack of opportunities for play and praise are social blights which have to be removed. We are shocked by instances of child abuse yet fail to remove the social conditions which so often may cause that abuse and which, no matter how caring the parents may be, deny children their birthright to full growth and development. By the same token, if we also believe all the evidence of the importance of these early years in the intellectual development of children, we must also provide adequately for their early, pre-school education and social development.

We have indicated some of the salient features of a good nursery education. Howe (1990b) reviews the research evidence for what can sensibly be done by parents to foster children's development whilst avoiding the excesses and the exaggerated claims of the advocates of hot-housing, the intensive early education of young children. What he has to say is important both for parents and for all concerned with education, whether as teachers or administrators. He is in no doubt that research confirms that talking with children and early reading to children is vitally important and accelerates their language development. He rightly stresses the following ways of fostering language in infancy:

1. Baby responds most readily to high-pitched voices.
2. Speak with dramatic emphasis, with gestures and actions which point up meaning.
3. Play vocabulary games with baby to give plenty of repetition and fun with new words or concepts.
4. Keep language simple.
5. Whisper to encourage attentive listening and to play another language game.
6. Speak slowly.
7. Give children time to respond and to converse.
8. Use rhythm and rhyme.
9. Speak directly to children.
10. Match conversation to the children's mental activity.
11. Ask questions that encourage thinking.
12. Don't be too concerned about children's mistakes of pronunciation or grammar.

As children get older Howe emphasizes the importance of involving them in adult conversation and in talking *with* children as recommended by Wiener (1988). Howe's suggestions on the importance of early reading, one or two years in advance of normal, are supported by recommending Carol Baker's (1980) practical *Reading Through Play: The Easy Way to Teach Your Child* and our *Teach Your Child to Read* (Young and Tyre, 1985). So far as the development of specific skills in areas such as music and mathematics is concerned, Howe emphasizes the importance of early instruction, practice, motivation and the painstaking development of abilities and of the parents' involvement in fostering them. Wisely, he cautions that, 'while it is wrong to subject young children to regimes of early education that are too formal, narrow, or intense, there is every reason for parents to provide extra opportunities for learning'. He also makes the point that children of wealthy, influential parents are often greatly advantaged. As in all his writings, Howe stresses the primacy of nurture over nature:

> Many people still believe that the most impressive human accomplishments depend on certain innate talents or gits. If this were true, the implication would be that the best we can do is identify a child's talents as early as possible and help provide conditions that will nurture them. But that belief belongs to folklore, not science. When we are confronted with the substantial body of findings showing that the majority of children are born capable of acquiring impressive levels of expertise in most spheres of competence, it becomes clear that it is entirely realistic to encourage any normal child to master important basic skills considerably earlier than usual.

The danger of narrow and intense education is in the uneven development it may cause, as instanced by John Stuart Mill, Norbert Wiener and John Ruskin, and the difficulty they had in adjusting to adult life. As we discuss elsewhere, we should at all times allow adequate time for play, space for individual choice and decision making, opportunities for being with one's peers and a broad social and cultural life. There are, however, proper limits to what parents can and should provide. The infant prodigy should not be allowed to be the cuckoo in the nest. On the other hand, Howe points out that in many fields, such as music, mathematics and tennis, starting early, receiving the best possible tuition and the development of a sense of commitment are distinct, often essential, advantages. Without the advantages of wealth and privilege, it is surprising that so many children succeed in realizing their potential. Perhaps there is some truth in Francis Bacon's, 'Prosperity doth best discover vice, but adversity doth best discover virtue'.

Nursery education has a vital part to play in helping children to make an early start in social, intellectual, physical and cultural development. For gifted children, good part-time nursery education may well counterbalance their concentration upon the development of their specific skills. Bad, unstructured and undemanding nursery education extraordinarily able children will find extraordinarily boring and an unwelcome distraction. It is possible to disagree with Howe's rather muddled semantics when he dismisses giftedness on the one hand and readmits it on the other as 'there is evidence that babies do differ, even in the earliest months of life, in ways that in some cases may – indirectly and via a chain of causes and effects – have effects on their eventual patterns of adult abilities'. It is a pity, too, that he fails to draw parents' attention to the wide range of abilities and differences children may have and the many ways in which they may be developed. But there is no gainsaying the importance he attaches to early education and his urging that 'it is entirely realistic to encourage any normal child to master important basic skills considerably earlier than usual'. The cooperation of parents and teachers in these early years is, perhaps, the best possible investment society can make provided it is prepared to build upon the abilities of children. What our society has not recognized is that failure to develop the abilities of the majority of our children accounts for their boredom, sense of alienation, anomie or frustration. Their education is neither appropriate to their abilities nor to the needs of society.

Dangers of Hot-housing

1. Parental anxiety will make the child over-anxious.
2. Pressure will make the child feel inadequate and tense.
3. Living through one's child subordinates the child's needs.
4. Insistence on performance and correctness will make the child afraid to fail.
5. Children who are afraid to fail will avoid performing.
6. Concentration on early formal learning is inappropriate to a child's developmental learning strategies.
7. Over-loaded programmes limit opportunities for rest and play.
8. An over-loaded programme will limit opportunities for mixing with similar peers and with those less and more able than self.
9. An over-concentration on academic abilities will reduce opportunities for achievement in areas in which children may be gifted, inhibit curiosity and stress conformity.
10. Over-concentration on the child's gifts will inhibit all-round development essential for full realization of potential.
11. Exploiting young children's dependence upon adults and their compliance and eagerness to please may result in their ultimate rebellion and rejection of parental or adult values.
12. Early gains may be at the cost of personal and social adjustment difficulties later in life.

Children's resilience and eagerness to please may mask early feelings of anxiety and parents and teacher should be on the alert for signs of stress, such as disturbed sleep, task avoidance, nail-biting, hair-pulling, depression, tiredness, under-achievement, boredom, tearfulness and an inability to make friends.

Tutoring in the Pre-school Years

An alternative parents may consider is that of tutoring for their children in the pre-school years if they feel that they are not able to meet their demands to learn more. If we take the example of the good music teacher or athletics coach whose lessons provide a model of mastery, encouragement and enthusiasm, instruction and performance by the child of what has been practised between lessons, we can see that a teacher of maths, science or a foreign language, say, can achieve a great deal in one or two short sessions each week. If the parent is actively involved in the lessons, so much the better. Between lessons, the parent is now able to help with the practice, repeat instruction and clear up any misunderstandings. The Suzuki method of violin teaching involves parents in this way.

The nature and quality of instruction needs to be similar to that which we have discussed as the interactive mode of parental education, although there will now possibly be more structure. If children respond with enthusiasm to their lessons and look forward to them, parents will know that all is well. If, after an initial period of adjustment, the lessons are resisted and it is clear little or no progress is being made, then they should be abandoned. Talented musicians find that if the relationship between teacher and pupil is poor, lessons can be counterproductive. The ability to communicate enthusiasm and the skill to lead the pupil forward step by step with STRING (Short-Term Realizable INteresting Goals) are the hallmarks of the successful coach, tutor, lecturer, instructor, teacher and parent alike. It may well be that for the normal academic subjects, qualified teachers are available, but today, with our ageing population and early retirement, there are many people with the time, interest and enthusiasm to teach bright children their own knowledge and skills. They are a resource which is badly underused. The advantages of one-to-one learning cannot be over-estimated. This may be the beginning of the mentor method most gifted children come to thrive on.

Power Amplifiers of Thought

When children learn that Fido is a dog and dogs are dogs and not cats or fish, or that tables and chairs are furniture, they are learning that things can be classified. The concept is one of the building blocks of science, the beginnings of classification and taxonomies. When they learn disparate things can be described as belonging to the same set of shapes, that wheels, eyes, cups and the planet have circles in common, or that fields can be pasture, playing, frozen and magnetic, their thinking becomes more powerful because they are no longer limited to think in terms solely of function but in abstractions. Similarly, when they learn the associative, commutative, conservative, reversability and distributive properties of number they are learning more than the basic laws of mathematics and beginning their understanding of logic. Making a simple plan or using a microscope gives children experience of proportion. Playing a scale is more than a finger exercise – it is the introduction of the concepts of harmony and key; the conventions of bars and quavers introduce musical time and rhythm. Weighing on a scale introduces the physics of mass and equilibria.

These amplifiers of thought, as Bruner (1972) has described them, are factors in our culture, key concepts, which extend our understanding and interpretation of our universe and enable us to think more accurately and cogently. The Arabic number system amplified our mathematical abilities. Newtonian mechanics, such as his law that acceleration = force divided by mass, amplified Aristotelian mechanics and was in turn amplified by quantum mechanics.

By patterning and chunking – recoding information so that we can more readily remember it – we can become more skilful as musicians, surgeons, sportsmen and women and in the vast range of activities from lace-making to engineering. We can hold long and complex sequences in our minds and our bodies can execute them. But, like learning to think, learning to perform has to be learned and, for the most part, has to be taught. Imitation may well assist the process, but training and practice accelerate acquisition of intellectual and physical skills.

In our concern to develop the potential abilities of children, as parents and teachers we need to be aware of the potency of these amplifiers of thought. At King's College, London, Shayer, Adey and Yates have been working on a 7-year project to develop the reasoning abilities of 14-year-olds and have identified 10 basic processes: *classification, ratio, proportion, variables, exclusion of variables, correlation, probability, multiplicative compensation, equilibria* and *using abstract models*. They have taught comprehensive school mixed-ability first- and second-year pupils these thinking strategies in carefully structured science lessons which encourage cognitive conflict, attempting to resolve conflicting ideas, the application of thinking strategies to different situations, and metacognition, thinking about thinking. In one school, nearly half of the experimental group pupils gained grade C or above in GCSE maths and science, and all the grade As were gained by experimental group pupils. None of the non-experimental group pupils got As and fewer gained Bs, only 28 per cent of them gaining C or above. In another school, the experimental group achieved higher results in GCSE English.

Reuven Feuerstein (1979), who argues that 'It is not the culture of the individual that is depriving but it is the fact that the individual is deprived of his own culture that is the disabling factor', believes that if parents have been unable to pass on society's culture, then the children can be helped by Mediated Learning Experience (MLE) given by specially trained teachers using Instrumental Enrichment. The purpose is to change the pupils' thinking and their ability to understand their world. Like Vygotsky's Zone of Proximal Development (ZPD), Feuerstein's Learning Potential Assessment Device (LPAD) uses tests not to measure abilities of pupils but to discover the blocks and gaps in their thinking so that they may be overcome.

Concrete Experience

The advantages that those children learning an instrument have over those children learning academic subjects are that the musicians have immediate feedback of what they are doing and that they are learning concretely and enactively. Feedback and knowledge of results are valuable in all learning. They tell us, if we are right, that we can continue and, if we are wrong, that we should carry out the necessary corrections. Without immediate knowledge of results, a child 'doing' a page of sums may well repeat the same error and thereby reinforce it. But the big advantage is that the musician or athlete is learning concretely. Concrete experience prepares the way for learning abstractions. The girl cutting out a skirt is making a truncated cone. If, as too rarely happens, she is given both the experience and the vocabulary, she will benefit from the experience cognitively and mathematically. One of the steps we need to take to realize children's potential is to give them this concrete experience across the curriculum and the language and thought amplifiers or key concepts to enable them to use it. The musician who is learning the fingering and the dexterity with the neuromuscular automatization of scale or phrase playing will in turn be helped by studying harmony.

As mentioned earlier, concrete experience of mathematics begins in infancy, and parents and teachers need to develop and extend this approach to learning first in everyday real-life situations and then across the curriculum. It is essential, however, to supply the language and the concepts so that children can think within the structures of the disciplines. Street arithmetic works and is thoroughly efficient and appropriate for the purposes, such as betting or trading, for which it was devised. As we shall see in Chapter 7, it appears that some of the extraordinary people who calculate the days of the week on which events took place use similar strategies. We have known street-sharp children in inner-city schools who were adept at calculations in their weekend and holiday jobs in the market but almost innumerate in school. They were not lacking in ability nor in experience, but education had failed to build upon either. They illustrate both what Feuerstein maintains and what we have been urging for the realization of the potential of all children.

Exceptionally able children, exposed to rich concrete and cultural experience, are able to stride ahead because they have been equipped with these tools of thought. They are able to apply what they have learned to other situations and to think for themselves. They demonstrate that they can go beyond the information given, have large zones of proximal development and are both curious and active learners. They have enjoyed the process which has been in harmony with their development and the pleasure of the success it has given them. Thus they have become intrinsically motivated to learn more. All this has contributed to their learning set or positive attitude to learning. In the process, they have acquired self-discipline.

What We Mean by Discipline

> Mary has long legs and a trim, fit body. She has already won the under-thirteens' 100 metres in house and school events. She's been entered for the area sports and enjoys running. She's joined the local athletics club and attends one evening a week and every Saturday morning for coaching. She runs every morning before school. All this gives her a healthy appetite and her coach has given her a diet sheet. This year she has equalled the county record and is county junior champion. Her friends say she was sure to win – she's got long legs, like her mother. It makes Mary angry.

> When Alan Sillitoe was invalided out of the RAF he decided he wanted to write. He went abroad to eke out his small pension and wrote and wrote until he'd written a novel based on the life he knew in Nottingham. The book was rejected. He wrote it again and again, honing his prose and sharpening his narrative. After years of writing and rewriting his novel was accepted. When *Saturday Night and Sunday Morning* was published the critics hailed him as a natural born writer. It made Alan Sillitoe angry.

It is easy to ignore the effort and discipline involved in achieving success and to attribute the results to inherited abilities, to the predestination of genes. It is equally fallacious to put attainment down solely to hard work, favoured circumstances or an over-weaning drive for success. One of the key factors in achievement is that, in the process of becoming self-motivated, children learn to be disciplined. This is not discipline in the sadistic sense, as was the case with the floggings Tennyson received from his headmaster which, on one occasion, put him in bed for 6 weeks, or the kicks on the shins Puccini received whenever he played a wrong note so that, for the rest of his life, the sound of a wrong note caused his fist to jerk up and stab the air. Nor do we mean unquestioning obedience to others.

By discipline we mean a willingness to learn and a preparedness to accept that to do so may entail subordinating one's own wishes and predilections to others. This may mean accepting previously tried and tested procedures, such as the need to practise or to reflect before making assertions. The subjects of the curriculum are rightly called disciplines because they contain established procedures, hierarchies of classification, knowledge and skills which need to be learned. When Picasso was in his surrealist period, he surprised many people when, on being asked what was the best training for a surrealist painter, replied, 'A traditional, academic training.' He went on to acknowledge the need for mastery of all the techniques and knowledge which had been built up over the centuries in order that they could be at the disposal of the artist's imagination.

The psychologist David Ausubel (1968) describes the concept of discipline we are advocating as applied to the school setting, but it is equally appropriate to the familial one and, for 'teachers' and 'classroom', 'parents' and 'home' may be substituted. His concept, too, fits nicely into the apprenticeship model:

> Democratic discipline is as rational, nonarbitrary, and bilateral as possible. It provides explanations, permits discussion, and invites the participation of children in the setting and enforcement of standards whenever they are qualified to do so. Above all it implies respect for the dignity of the individual, makes its primary appeal to self-control, and avoids exaggerated emphasis on status differences and barriers between free communication. Hence it repudiates harsh, abusive and vindictive forms of punishment and the use of sarcasm, ridicule and intimidation . . . This type of discipline also becomes increasingly more feasible as children become older, more responsible, more capable of self-control and group control, and more capable of understanding and formulating rules of conduct based on concepts of equity and reciprocal obligation. But contrary to what the extreme permissivists would have us believe, democratic school discipline does not imply freedom from all constraints, standards and direction, or freedom from discipline. And under no circumstances does it presuppose the eradication of all distinctions between pupil and teacher roles, or require that teachers abdicate responsibility for making the final decisions in the classroom.

Gifted children need the security of this rational discipline and their parents and teachers need to encourage the development of their self-discipline and self-motivation without the excesses of obsessiveness which may sometimes arise. This concept of discipline provides a framework in which we can ensure that a balance is kept between those activities about which children are enthusiastic and those which are essential to their progress and all-round education and maturity but about which they are less keen. Certainly, without self-discipline, potential cannot be realized in the scientific, artistic, athletic, literary or any other field. It is discipline which distinguishes between the professional and the dilettante, between accomplishment and dabbling. The difference between natural beauty and the beauty of a work of art, is the work.

It is clear by now that realizing children's potential is demanding. We said at the outset that we regard successful parenting as the most creative achievement of all human endeavours. Yehudi Menuhin (1977), whose upbringing has been criticized by some with less sensitivity and insight than he displays, has this to say:

> To raise a gifted child is not unlike raising a cretin, I imagine. The exorbitant demands it makes can neither be ignored nor be reduced to normal measures, and the special concentration it attracts necessarily overturns ordinary priorities . . . But for all that, I believe my sisters and I would have been the objects of no less care and organization had we never played a note.

If we are to realize the potential of all our children, then parents need the support of their extended families, so far as they are able, and of the community as a whole. The Menuhins were supported by their grandparents and in order to educate their children rejected local education and provided tutors for them. Few families can do this. But, if we examine more closely what it is that makes prodigies, geniuses, gifted people, high achievers, champions or medallists, we may be better able to increase their number dramatically.

CHAPTER 6

Creators and Creativity

A Proper Study

If the proper study of mankind is man and, as Bacon held, 'histories make men wise', it is entirely appropriate that there has always been an interest in geniuses and prodigies. The word 'genius', from the Latin *gens* (= family) and the term genius, meaning 'begetter', comes from the early Roman cult of a divinity as the head of the family. In its earliest form, genius was concerned with the ability of the head of the family, the *paterfamilias*, to perpetuate himself. The feminine counterpart was Juno. Gradually, genius came to represent a person's characteristics and thence an individual's highest attributes derived from his genius or guiding spirit. Identifying and worshipping the emperor's genius developed from this. Today, people still look to stars or genes, astrology or genetics, in the hope of finding the source of exceptional abilities or personal characteristics.

The history of civilization in all cultures abounds with examples of oral and written tramsmission of stories of the genealogies and lives of their leaders, heroes and saints. Significantly, too, many religions tell of a search for or discovery of a baby, a Jesus, Moses, Mohammed, Dalai Lama or Hiawatha, to lead them. Today, the media record the minute details of the lives of the famous and the achievements of prodigies in chess, gymnastics, bravery, music and academic attainment.

The concept of genius and of gifts has become part of our folk culture and attitudes are ambivalent towards them. We envy the gifted and mistrust them. In the mythology of giftedness, it is popularly believed that if people are talented in one area they must be defective in another, that intellectuals are impractical, that prodigies burn too brightly too soon and burn out, that gifted people are eccentric, that they are physical weaklings, that there's a thin line between genius and madness, that genius runs in families, that the gifted are so clever they don't need special help, that giftedness is the same as having a high IQ, that some races are more intelligent or musical or mathematical than others, that genius goes unrecognized and unrewarded, that adversity makes men wise or that people with gifts have a responsibility to use them. Language has been enriched with such terms as high-brow, egghead, blue-stocking, wiseacre, know-all, boffin and, for many, intellectual is a term of denigration.

It was not always so. The Renaissance saw the burgeoning of the universal man, of the da Vincis and Albertis whose abilities transcended other men's or who were multi-talented and were inspired by Manetti's humanist watchword, *agere et intelligere*, to do and to understand. Giorgio Vasari's *Lives* gave the biographies of 200 painters, sculptors and architects, chief among them that of Michaelangelo.

It is not surprising to find that in Victorian England, with its belief in human perfectability, there was both a flowering of talent and considerable interest in the nature of genius. Francis Galton, himself a genius who could read before he was 3 and studied Latin at 4, trained as a physician, travelled in Africa and published the results of his explorations before turning his attention to meteorology in which he established the technique of weather mapping. After his first cousin Charles Darwin published his *On the Origin of Species by Natural Selection* (1859), Galton devoted himself to the study of heredity, demonstrated the individuality of fingerprints and set up the system for their identification and classification. In 1869, he published his study of *Hereditary Genius*, in 1874 his *English Men of Science* and in 1883 *Inquiries into Human Faculty and Its Development*. He founded eugenics and, although he was unaware of Mendel's work in genetics, he was seriously concerned to understand how heredity worked and how human abilities and characteristics could be improved.

John Stuart Mill records in his *Autobiography* (1873) how his father, James, educated him, beginning with Greek at age 3. However, he always insisted that John understood everything he learned and never permitted his studies to degenerate into mere rote learning. Although his education was broadly based and John was a willing and able learner, he was isolated from other children and the process was demanding and not without its pains. Moreover, he found great difficulty in finding his own identity and independence. That he eventually outshone his Utilitarian father both in his career in the India House and as a philosopher and economist is testimony to his own genius.

In Austria, Karl Witte was also working on the other side of the nature–nurture equation with a system of education to produce prodigies. The method certainly made his son a brilliant scholar and an authority on Dante. Norbert Wiener, the founder of cybernetics, was educated by his father, a polyglot and famous scholar, on Witte's principles, which he translated. Norbert Wiener entered Tufts University at 11 and gained his doctorate at Harvard at the age of 18. Like Mill, Wiener relates in his 'The autobiography of an ex-prodigy' (1953) the difficulties he had in growing up and establishing his independence.

In Italy, the criminologist Cesare Lombroso was working on his studies of genius at Turin University. Published in 1888 under the title, *L'Uomo di genio* and in England as *The Man of Genius* (1891), Lombroso's contribution to the subject was to emphasize the peculiarities of genius and to regard it as a form of deviation from the norm and, therefore, a form of degeneracy. He listed the geniuses who were short, deformed and, phrenology and classification by head size and shape being in vogue, had big or misshapen heads. Perhaps one of the more interesting observations he made was that so few of his geniuses had children and how many were celibate. But the major influence of Lombroso's work was to add weight to the romantic myth of genius as troubled and close to madness.

Early investigators of genius, such as Lombroso, took as their criterion of genius the fame of their subjects. Havelock Ellis, for his *A Study of British Genius* (1904), used a similar standard: he selected those who had three or more pages devoted to them in the recently published *Dictionary of National Biography*, 1030 (975 men, 55 women) out of 30 000 entries. He was particularly interested in their precocity, whether in the form of early general ability, early specialization of interests or physical activities, but observed that it was rare for originality or real achievements to be made until after adolescence. It is interesting to note that, in his autobiography, *My Life*, Ellis (1939) relates how, during his own adolescence in Australia he made careful measurements of his growth and found that he was taller in the morning than at night, as if he'd shrunk slightly during the day, a phenomenon he only found confirmed many years later in a medical journal.

Perhaps, for us today, one of the most significant aspects of most of these studies of genius is the frequency with which early encouragement and teaching by parents and tutors had beneficial effects on the intellectual, artistic or musical development of the children but caused great difficulties of adjustment later in their lives, and the frequency with which abilities went unrecognized by teachers and schools. However, the difficulty about the evidence produced by these studies, fascinating as they are in collecting together anecdotes and apparent similarities and exceptions, is that they are not what we would today call norm-referenced. In other words, when, for instance, information is collated about early illnesses, methods of upbringing, schooling, etc., we must also take into account information from other historical sources about how common or exceptional these were at the time. For instance, infant mortality was high and life expectancy much shorter than today, home tutoring was common in the families of the nobility and wealthy, bullying and corporal punishment were common at the best independent schools and, in the overwhelming majority of cases, the subjects studied were members of the privileged classes. It was only with the growth of paediatrics and psychology that studies could be carried out on a more objective if not always very scientific basis.

Genuises, however they are defined, if selected retrospectively whether from Nobel Prize winners, from the memberships of scientific societies or from the Pantheon of past composers and artists, are but the peaks which stand out through the mist of history and are visible to the particular observer from his or her particular vantage point. Change the observers and the vantage points, clear away some of the mist, and a different lot of peaks appear. And what of all the other able men and women who fell foul of the corporate orthodoxy of the medical, scientific or academic establishments of their time, and have been consigned to obscurity until, perhaps, a few have their worth rediscovered and re-evaluated?

Genius is a term we apply to those whom we recognize as having made outstanding achievements and who stand near the end of the continuum of human abilities which reaches back through the mundane and mediocre to the disabled and incapable. There is still much truth in Dr Samuel Johnson's, 'The true genius is a mind of large general powers, accidentally determined to some particular direction.' We may disagree with the 'general', for we doubt if all musicians of genius could have become scientists of genius or vice versa, but there is no doubting the accidental determination which nurtured or triggered their gifts into those channels into which they have poured their powers so successfully.

Along the continuum of abilities are hundreds of thousands of gifted men and women, boys and girls. Some, like Goethe, who investigated the physics of light, geology, and the structure of plants and bones – he coined the term 'morphology' – have large general powers. Others, like Dylan Thomas or Pablo Casals, have a specific talent. Some will be extraordinarily gifted, some will have but modest gifts. There will be great gifts squandered or under-developed and small gifts lavishly rewarded. It is fatuous to divorce genius or giftedness from the real world and to believe that they represent some different form of neurological endowment from that enjoyed or endured by the rest of us. There is no difference of form, only a difference of degree. As Coleridge recognized, it was 'myriad-minded' Shakespeare's intellect which 'seems forever twisting and untwisting its own strength' which gave his work its universality.

What we appreciate, enjoy or marvel at in the works of genius or the achievements of prodigies, are the manifestations of skills or abilities which are similar to, but so much superior to, our own. But that their minds are not different from our own is demonstrated by the fact that the hard won discoveries of a Kepler or Einstein become the commonplace knowledge of schoolchildren and the once outrageous shapes and colours of a Paul Klee so soon appear on the fabrics we wear. This does not minimize the supremacy of their achievements which outstrip our own as the sub-four minute milers outstrip our jogging.

To think of geniuses and the gifted as having uniquely different brains is only reasonable if we accept that each human brain is uniquely different. What we must also accept is that the purpose of training or instruction is to make us even more different from one another. In the process of being educated, we are exposed to the achievements of those more gifted than ourselves and learn from them. Some prodigies may overtake both their mentors and models. We can also learn from the example of the gifted and, by studying their techniques, strategies and processes, discern something of how they succeeded so outstandingly – and, maybe, avoid some of their mistakes. Studies of gifted mathematical or musical pupils may inform the training of ordinary pupils. All of us can gain something from examining the lives of geniuses, but before we try to emulate them or encourage our children to do so we should note that some of the things we learn from them may prove unpalatable. We may envy their achievements and fame, but we should also recognize the price they may have paid in terms of perseverance, single-mindedness, dedication, restrictions on their personal lives, the demands upon their energies and time, and how often they had to display great courage to preserve their integrity or to make their way to the top.

In our examination of giftedness, its nature and realization, we should keep these demands in the front of our minds. No matter how gifted children may be, they are still children and children are not little adults. They must be educated not only in their gifted abilities and related areas but as children with all the emotional, social, physical and other developing and changing needs of children. Failure to do this may well produce a warped but talented, able but miserable misfit. Research and common sense make it clear that that need not be so and is, in any case, counterproductive in every way. The essence of the education of gifted children is that they should enjoy all that they do and be motivated by their own achievements while leading full and rewarding lives with their peers as well as with those with similar abilities and talents. This again, of course, is what we want for all children.

Genius and giftedness are relative descriptive terms of no real substance. We may, at best, give them some precision by defining them and placing them in a context but, whatever we do, we should never delude ourselves into believing that gifted children or geniuses are different from the rest of humanity save in the degree to which they have developed the performance of their abilities.

We define a genius as someone who has made a unique contribution to our understanding of the universe or of ourselves or to our enjoyment and perception of them. This definition includes scientists, philosophers, mathematicians and writers, artists, composers and performers. It is characteristic of the works of genius in any field that they have universality and longevity. The discoveries of Kepler, Newton or Einstein may well be superseded by later discoveries, but the uniqueness and significance of their work remain as significant benchmarks in the evolution of man's exploration, thinking and understanding of our universe. Similarly, fashions in the arts may change and new skills and techniques be developed, but the works of geniuses will continue to be remembered and reappraised by succeeding generations. In some instances, it may well be that works of genius will not be universally recognized as such when they are first revealed before an unsuspecting world because they are so far in advance of their time or because they appear to have no practical application or significance, as in the case of Boole's algebra which had no practical application until the development of computers, or of Van Gogh's paintings. What scientists or artists do is to make or create things, performances or ideas, and the study of how they do so has given rise in psychology to the study of what is called 'creativity'.

What We Mean by Creativity

Creativity is a term we use with some reluctance and we would prefer to limit its use to that supreme act of creation, the birth of a child and its parenting to maturity and independence as a life-enhancing contributor to society. If this were seen as the miracle it is and given proper esteem, we would value women and children more highly than most societies do and the world would be a better place. But the term is bandied about to cover everything from the creation of the universe to flower arranging. We would certainly prefer to use terms such as inventiveness, origination, making, discovering, insightfulness, perceptiveness, innovation or problem solving. Not only are such terms more specific, they need not be hierarchical, although attempts have been made to arrange them in order. It is reasonable to distinguish between the inventiveness of Leonardo da Vinci's drawings of submarines and flying-machines, the perceptiveness of his anatomical drawings and the insightfulness of his studies of inertia, without suggesting that one act was better than the others or that they were all simply creative. Moreover, none of them would have received the fascinated attention of generations if he had not been such a great draughtsman.

As early as 1926, Graham Wallas developed the ideas of von Helmholtz about how scientific discoveries are made. Helmholtz, one of the greatest physicists of the nineteenth century, for instance, had been fascinated by Faraday's apparent intuitive ability to find general theorems, 'the methodical deductions of which requires the highest powers of mathematical analysis', without the help of a single mathematical formula. Wallas suggested that there were four steps in the creative process:

• *Preparation*: investigating the problem, gathering relevant data.
• *Incubation*: consciously getting away from the problem and waiting.
• *Illumination*: the sudden insight or breakthrough when the solution comes.
• *Verification*: evaluating and testing the solution before applying it.

In mathematics, Polya's *How To Solve It* (1971) revived heuristic, the contraction of 'heuristic method', the study of the processes and rules of invention and discovery which had been largely neglected since the attempts of Descartes, Leibnitz and Bernard Bolzano to build up a system. Modern heuristic is important in cybernetics and computer design, but the procedures described by Polya are of value to students of mathematics, the physical and social sciences alike, and we shall discuss them in more detail below.

Irving Taylor (1959) suggested five levels of creativity which he considered appropriate to both artistic and scientific activities:

1. *Expressive*: where skill, originality, quality of execution are unimportant.
2. *Productive*: skilled execution.
3. *Inventive*: the discovery of new, unusual relationships.
4. *Innovative*: modifying the basis or principles of science or art.
5. *Emergentive*: finding fundamentally new principles of science or art.

One may readily apply these terms to the developing work of a child or art student, who might never attain the innovative and emergentive levels. Similarly, they could describe the progress of a scientist as he studies the work of his peers, tests their hypotheses, and invents a new application of them, as in the case of Marconi when he used Hertz's method of producing radio waves and developed a 'coherer' to detect them; later, he was innovative when he discovered that radio waves followed the earth's curvature and didn't radiate straight outwards. Whether his successful work of transmitting signals from Land's End to Newfoundland is 'innovative' or 'emergentive', however, is a matter of opinion, depending upon one's perspective: technologically, it might well be emergentive, but in terms of pure science his work does not mark the finding of a new principle such as Kamerlingh-Onnes's discovery of superconductivity in 1911. In literature and art, opinions are always likely to differ as to how creative and particularly how innovative and emergentive writers and artists may have been. Who was the more emergentive 'stream of consciousness' writer – Dorothy Richardson or James Joyce? But it is certainly preferable to use these discrete terms than to use 'creative' indiscriminately.

Koestler (1964), in his detailed and perceptive study of the creative process in humour, science, literature and art, suggests that it is the ability to make bisociative leaps from one frame of reference to another, with which it is not usually associated, which characterizes the creative thinking of genius. It is this which connects Archimedes' 'Eureka!' on discovering the principle of buoyancy with Ampère's 'cry of joy' when he suddenly solved the problem of probability which had puzzled him for 7 years. Similarly, the dream of a snake biting its own tail enabled August von Kekulé to lay one of the cornerstones of modern science, rings of carbon atoms and the structure of benzene, discovered by Faraday. Kekulé's subsequent advice to colleagues 'Let us learn to dream' and the popular wisdom which advises us 'to sleep on it' is in turn connected with Coleridge's account of how he came to write *Kubla Khan* – a waking dream induced by two grains of opium to check dysentery, and with the rhythmic beat which Yeats said, 'lulls the mind into a waking trance'.

The significance of these insights into creative acts is that they provide descriptions of states with which we are all familiar and that they demonstrate that, in these moments of inspiration, scientists and artists are regressing to earlier stages of cerebration. They are, in Koestler's words, 'thinking aside'. As Woodworth wrote, 'Often we have to get away from speech in order to think clearly', and it is then that, in regressing, we prepare for a leap forward, *reculer pour mieux sauter*. The existence of these pre-conscious states, noted by John Norris (1657–1711), Leibnitz, Kant, Hegel, Goethe, Fichte, W.B. Carpenter, and by Wordsworth with his 'caverns in the mind which sun can never penetrate', is recognized by Maudsley (in Whyte, 1962): 'The most important part of mental action, the essential process on which thinking depends, is unconscious mental activity.' Wundt (ibid.) put it more dramatically: 'The unconscious mind is for us like an unknown being who creates and produces for us, and finally throws the ripe fruits in our lap.'

But serendipity favours the informed mind and it is only when the accumulated skills and knowledge have been mastered that the mind is freed and able to make these cognitive leaps. Koestler instances the contrast between the learning process of the pianist, who practises until the piece is memorized and he can 'play it in his sleep', with the creative process of Tartini composing the 'Devil's Trill Sonata' in his sleep. Eindhoven and Vinacke (1952), in their study of painters, confirmed Graham Wallas' analysis of the four stages of creativity – preparation, incubation, illumination and verification – but indicated that they found not four distinct stages but an ongoing dynamic process of their interplay.

Koestler, moreover, is concerned to examine the intellectual characteristics of scientific geniuses which he identifies as (1) precociousness, (2) scepticism and credulity, (3) abstraction and practicality and (4) multiple potential. For example, most scientists tend to confirm the popular belief about precociousness and peak early, performing their best work before age 40 although they may well not distinguish themselves at school. This is because their precocity may be masked by boredom and by scepticism about the received wisdom of teachers and lecturers (the rubbish with which Einstein complained he had to stuff himself for examinations) and by credulity – as when he fantasised that he was travelling at the speed of light. While scientists may think in the abstractions of their disciplines for much of the time, they need a streak of practicality, to be able to recognize the facts of physical science; in Maxwell's words, 'when they meet them out-of-doors', or, like Faraday, the blacksmith's son, to make his own equipment for his experiments when necessary. Koestler quotes Galileo encouraging colleagues to learn natural philosophy from craftsmen in the real world, in the arsenals of Venice.

By multiple potential Koestler draws attention to the part chance plays in launching scientists on their careers. The bizarre chances which took Faraday from book-binding to succeeding his mentor Sir Humphry Davy as professor of chemistry at the Royal Institution and from establishing the laws of electrolysis and of electromagnetic induction to the publication of the seven volumes of his meticulously kept notebooks, are typical. We are reminded of Johnson's description 'of large general powers, accidentally determined to some particular direction, ready for all things but chosen by circumstances for one'. However, that one direction may lead scientists to solve a variety of problems, as in Faraday's case when he gave his attention to perfecting Davy's lamp, to electromagnetism, to the localization of the chemical industry or to the production of heat-resistant glass. It is as if the mind of the genius is capable of being sparked off to discharge its energy into a variety of problems.

Curiosity, an open but informed mind, and the energy and persistence to tackle apparently insoluble problems are characteristics of many great scientists and artists alike. Dickens, for all his prolific output of books, undertook exhausting lecture and dramatic tours, founded two weekly magazines, travelled widely in Europe and America, investigated a variety of social problems and campaigned for children's hospitals, the preservation of Shakespeare's birthplace and on behalf of Mechanics' Institutes. He had only a few years' rudimentary education and was 58 when he died. 'Genius does what it must, and Talent does what it can', as Owen Meredith, Earl of Lytton, modestly wrote.

Boden (1990) has related Koestler's conceptualization of the act of creation to current work on Artificial Intelligence (AI) and the connectionist approach to AI in particular. Her study demonstrates how far we have to go before the creations of AI can approach those of the child who writes a verse or cracks a joke.

Shaughnessy (1990), reviewing the contribution of recent theoretical analyses of the thinking processes which are thought to characterize giftedness, identifies the contributions of information theorists, Sternberg and Davidson's (1985) triarchic theory and Gardner's (1983) mutiple intelligence theory. Shaughnessy proposes a valuable synthesis of their findings in the form of what he calls 'a six realm domain for the understanding of cognitive-processing propensities of the gifted':

1. *Accelerated acquisition*: both of knowledge and between-stage acquisition of Piagetian constructs.
2. *Accelerated automatization*: the gifted child learns to perform rote mechanical operations quicker and processes information at deeper levels with greater rapidity.
3. *Automatic activation*: gifted thinkers more readily directly and indirectly activate componential processes (see Sternberg and Davidson, 1985) and access both indirect and direct feedback more readily than others.
4. There seems to be greater depth and propensity of emotive alignment. Thus, the young musician more readily chooses his or her instrument (violin), form of music (Renaissance concertos) and endears him or herself to that chosen domain more rapidly and strongly than other less inclined peers.
5. A secondary aspect of the above is intrinsic interest/inquisitiveness. This interest maintains the above emotive love for the subject areas and sustains long-term growth.
6. Finally, componential chunking or meta-analysis (or both) provides greater potential for problem solving, investigation and solution production, higher-order abstraction, evaluation and synthesis.

In effect, gifted children learn better and faster with greater insight, retain and use what they've learned, identify and identify with the subject area they most enjoy, are strongly intrinsically motivated and have greater abilities to solve problems and make cognitive leaps.

It is possible, too, to relate theories about the creative and problem-solving abilities of these children to Hudson's (1962, 1963) work on convergent and divergent thinking, to de Bono's (1970) vertical and lateral thinking, to Osborn's (1963) brainstorming techniques and to Gordon's (1961) 'synectics', which we will examine in more detail later. While they all provide insights into different aspects of cerebral activity, whether by analogy or by systematizing our thought processes, there is the real danger that we will come to think of creativity as a separate process, a specific function of the brain like memory or perception. Creativeness is an aspect of performance and it is as much a part of our everyday activity as our rational or irrational behaviour. What we have been examining are some of the characteristics of creativeness in the minds and activities of exceptionally able people. The processes themselves are not unique.

If we apply these behaviours to ourselves in our daily lives, we can all recognize the wisdom of standing back from problems, of kicking ideas around, of 'sleeping on things' and waking to find we have an unexpected solution, of being sceptical of the experts – whether they be doctors, politicians, economists or statisticians – and marshalling all the available facts before deciding on, say, the 'best buy'. We may also recognize that, but for chance circumstances, we may very well have used what abilities we have in a variety of quite different ways: we are all, to some extent, multi-directional. It is all a matter of degree. We need to remember this when thinking of our children and their education. If it is all a matter of degree, we need again Makarenko's 'sense of the mean'.

Koestler, throughout his work, argues against a mechanistic, behaviourist view of man. He dubbed behaviourism, with its rats running mazes and Pavlovian conditioning, 'ratomorphic' psychology. We should similarly beware of making too much of comparisons of our brains and their functions with telephone exchanges, positive and negative feedback systems or computer and information technology. Because we have made these tools, it isn't surprising that they reflect something of our make-up, just as a hammer is something like our fist. It is vital that we use our understanding of how genius performs to facilitate our children's growth and development and avoid, as far as is humanly possible, the difficulties, the 'slings and arrows of outrageous fortune', which some of them unnecessarily endured. If our children are educated according to their aptitudes and abilities, and if their educational and other needs are met, then we will have no need to worry about either their intelligence quotients or their creativity. In the USA, much research has focused on models of mental abilities in which creativity, as convergent and divergent production, is seen as one of its components (Guilford, 1967). Unfortunately for some, this has been seen as a biological model which is as deterministic as the ratomorphic psychology of the behaviourists. The behaviourists argued that we were conditioned by our environment; the intelligence testers argued that our abilities are determined by our genes (Jensen, 1969; Eysenck, 1971). The resultant controversy with claims and counterclaims of sexism and racism has demonstrated, if proof were needed, that the faults lie, 'But in ourselves, that we are underlings'. The biologists' response to these unscientific posturings is best summed up by Rose *et al.* (1984):

> What characterizes human development and actions is that they are the consequence of an immense array of interacting and intersecting causes. Our actions are not at random or independent with respect to the totality of those causes as an intersecting system, for we are material beings in a causal world. But to the extent that they are free, our actions are independent of any one or even a small subset of those multiple paths of causation: that is the precise meaning of freedom in a causal world . . . Our brains, hands, and tongues have made us independent of many single major features of the external world. Our biology has made us into creatures who are constantly re-recreating our own psychic and material environments, and whose individual lives are the outcomes of an extraordinary multiplicity of intersecting causal pathways. Thus it is our biology that makes us free.

It is this which makes Johnson's words about 'a mind of large general powers accidentally determined to some particular direction' and the emphasis on the scepticism, curiosity and multiple potentials of genius so important. Genius demonstrates not our predestination by inheritance nor our conditioning by our environment, but our freedom to choose how to explore and how to re-create our world. This being the case, the narrower their education, the earlier their specialization, and the less our gifted children are likely to be able to achieve. The deeper their education, the wider and richer their experience, and the better prepared and the more adaptable they will be.

Intelligence and Creativity

In the USA, where, following on the racist and sexist controversy referred to earlier, intelligence testing has been banned in many states, far greater attention has been given to creativity, to testing it and to teaching it. An important study by Getzels and Jackson (1962) was the first to highlight the significance being attached to creativity. They divided pupils in the University of Chicago Laboratory School, a private school for pupils with average IQs of 130, into two groups: the most intelligent children, and children with lower IQs who scored high on creativity. They reported that the highly creative pupils performed as well as the pupils with higher intelligence, were less conformist, had a high sense of humour and came from less academic families. Later, Wallach and Kogan (1965) compared pupils with high and low IQs and high and low creativity scores. They described their results, which might well serve as a warning about the tests and the whole intelligence–creativity controversy, as follows:

> *High creativity–high intelligence*: These children can exercise within themselves both control and freedom, both adult-like and childlike kinds of behaviour.
>
> *High creativity–low intelligence*: These children are in angry conflict with themselves and with their school environment and are beset by feelings of unworthiness and inadequacy. In a stress-free context, however, they can blossom cognitively.
>
> *Low creativity–high intelligence*: These children can be described as 'addicted' to school achievement. Academic failure would be conceived by them as catastrophic, so that they must continually strive for academic excellence in order to avoid the possibility of pain.
>
> *Low creativity–low intelligence*: Basically bewildered, these children engaged in various defensive manoeuvres ranging from useful adaptions such as intensive social activity to regressions such as passivity or psychosomatic symptoms.

These results, which omen ill for three-quarters of the tested population, have fortunately not been confirmed by other researchers and, as Wallach (1985) has pointed out, there is little evidence that the tests of ability or creativity predict achievement in real life. It is doubtful if creativity can be switched on in test conditions when we remember the importance of standing back from problems, the need for time for incubation. It is interesting to note that Burt (1964) perceptively recognized that:

> Educational psychologists have of late woken up to the fact that the kind of examinations and intelligence tests which they still habitually employ, tend to select the efficient learner and the verbal reasoner rather than the intuitive observers or constructive critical thinkers . . . Even when by some happy chance our methods of selection have picked out a potential inventor or budding genius, we still have no notion how he should be encouraged and instructed so as to develop to the utmost his unusual latent powers.

Today in Britain, tests of creativity are rarely used and intelligence testing is frequently regarded as being of value only as part diagnostic and part structured interview. Tests test what they have been designed to test and usually tell us more about the way in which the test designers think than about how those tested will perform in real life. If we want to know how fast someone can run we get them to run. If we want to know how much pupils can learn we have to begin by teaching them. Geniuses, however, operate at the frontiers of knowledge, grapple with problems which they alone, or in company with only a few others in the world at the time, have perceived. They have mastered all that is already known, have challenged it and gone beyond it.

The act of creation with which we have been concerned is a far cry from the concerns of those who have reduced creativity to a set of thinking skills. Creativity in any true sense of the word is developed in the process of mastering a discipline and is a fundamental and integral part of all problems in all subjects. Children who enjoy jokes, comic and nonsense verse, conundrums and riddles, puzzles and games of skill such as dominoes, computer games, draughts or chess, are already exercising many of the activities beloved of those who would teach them creativity. For this reason, it is the very fluidity of children's minds, their openness, credulity and playfulness which sensitive educators are anxious to preserve unblunted, along with their curiosity and sense of wonder, by the process of instruction. The gifted musician and mathematician both need to play. Here we are not thinking of the play-way approach to education akin to a year of wet playtimes but of 'genuine, pure play as one of the main bases of civilization'. In his *Homo Ludens*, Johan Huizinga (1970) defines play as:

> . . . an activity connected with no material interest, and no profit to be gained by it. It proceeds within its own proper boundaries of time and space according to fixed rules and in an orderly manner . . . as a contest for something or a representation of something. These two functions can unite in such a way that the game 'represents' a contest, or else becomes a contest for the best representation of something.

Huizinga argues that civilization 'arises *in* and *as* play and never leaves it' and demonstrates its central role in myth and religion, law, war, philosophy and art. The scientist or fashion designer 'toying' with ideas is engaging in the same kind of play in which we all indulge and it is essential that, in education, students of all ages are not kept in lock-step with rigid closed logic systems which allow no opportunities for their curiosity, independent thinking or exploratory drives. During infancy and adolescence, when pupils are most vulnerable to suggestion, if their curiosity is blunted and they are encouraged to believe that learning is no more than remembering what they have been told and regurgitating it on demand, we should not be surprised if they reject schooling and regard it as an irrelevant waste of their time. They will rapidly seek other areas for exploration.

We can teach a lot of science quickly by skipping through its 'laws', but if instead we allow time for exploratory activities we may find that some children, for example, will not be content to parrot that like poles repel and unlike poles attract and will try to find out what happens when they put numbers of bar magnets end to end. When studying the germination of seeds, one boy suggested that some of the specimens be rotated through 180° daily and an 8-year-old girl wanted to find out what would happen if some seeds were grown in a magnetic field. Just finding out what happens when or if is what science, art and technology are all about, and is a natural behaviour for all children.

Every school of psychology has its theory of play but, long before psychologists observed the play of apes, Darwin noted that 'All animals feel Wonder, and many exhibit Curiosity.' Pavlov's 'What is it?' reflex has been developed to explain how curiosity and exploration derive from the orienting reflex, the unlearned response to novelty and change, which may be reinforced or mediated: 'I like this banging noise' or 'It makes mummy cross'. Freudian theories regard play as substitute activities for unsatisfied urges and the resolution, through fantasy, of conflict and tensions. Erik Erikson (1950) sees play as the infantile form of creating model situations and mastering reality by experiment and planning and as a way of searching for identity in a particular milieu. Winnicott (1971) stresses the inherently exciting, precarious nature of play.

In his *Play, Dreams and Imitation in Childhood*, Jean Piaget (1951) identified three kinds of play in infancy for which adult behaviours may be readily substituted:

1. *Exercise play*: the repetition of an action for its own sake, not for understanding or practice, but for pleasure (vocalization in infancy; adults singing in the bath).
2. *Symbolic play*: structured behaviours in which there is representation of a reality not present (develops between 1½ and 3 years, playing mealtimes with dolls, leaves and stones; reading a novel).
3. *Rule play*: structured behaviours with others (from hide-and-seek to rugby or chess).

Observers of children's play have noted how socialization modifies play. A common classification shows the change which takes place around 4 years of age:

Under 3 years:
Solitary play
Parallel play – doesn't join in but plays beside others
Onlooker

Over 4 years:
Parallel play
Associative play
Cooperative play
Onlooker

Gifted children throughout their development need opportunities for these different kinds of play and they need them not only with similarly gifted peers but also with the generality of children and adults. Parents who indulge their children's enjoyment of solitary play with, say, their musical instruments or computers, and imagine that they are thus feeding their talent, may well be denying them the opportunity to develop and grow and to learn how to respond to others in the ordinary hurly-burly, rough-and-tumble of everyday life. Many gifted musicians who have grown up to fame and fortune complain, nevertheless, of feelings of isolation and of inadequacy in making relations. Jacqueline du Pré (Easton, 1989) explained her predicament as follows:

> 'It was a question of either/or. If you waited until schooling was finished to concentrate on music, it was about ten years too late.' . . . It (her cello) was her 'best friend', she said, 'until I was seventeen. No one who has not experienced it can know just what it means to have a private world of your own to go into, to be quiet by yourself whenever you need it. It was my gorgeous secret – an inanimate object, but I would tell it all my sadness and my problems. It gave me everything I needed and wanted. Playing was the cream. When I played, it never bothered me what happened. But I realized later that it didn't necessarily equip one to deal with one's fellow humans.'

For Jacqueline du Pré, for all her enormous vitality and sense of fun, solitary play had lasted too long. Parents and teachers need to provide escape from the rarified atmosphere of intense concentration upon mathematics or music in these early and adolescent years and to create a rich and balanced social and intellectual environment, the diversity of which stimulates interest and allows the developing child to find his or her personal identity. This can only be done in human, social relationships.

Carl Rogers (1959) emphasizes the importance of this openness to experience and the need for self-fulfilment, 'the tendency to express and activate all the capacities of the organism, to the extent that such activation enhances the organism or the self'. To be truly creative, which he defines as 'the emergence in action of a novel relational product, growing out of the uniqueness of the individual on the one hand, and the materials, events, people, or circumstances of his life on the other', Rogers identifies the following inner conditions:

- Openness to experience, flexibility in one's beliefs and perceptions.
- A tolerance of ambiguity.
- An internal locus of evaluation which recognizes others' views of one's work but doesn't let them alter it fundamentally.
- The ability 'to toy with' elements and concepts.
- Delight in intellectual exploration.

Rogers distinguishes between creativeness which is general and is concerned with self-realization and creativeness which is focused upon a specific gift. Maslow (1959) called these two senses of creativity, 'self-actualizing creativeness' and 'special talent creativeness'. The greater the former, the richer the latter. The more children realize their full potential as mature social beings, the happier they will be as adults. Maslow (1968) found that, in studies of the relationship between creativity and mental health, creative people are most likely to achieve self-actualization.

This openness to experience finds echoes in what Guilford identified in his model of intellect as the two kinds of productive abilities: convergent and divergent. The divergent factors he identified as being involved in creative thinking – word fluency, ideational fluency, semantic spontaneous flexibility, figural spontaneous flexibility, associational fluency, expressional fluency, symbolic adaptive flexibility, originality, elaboration – have encouraged many educators to emphasize the importance of fluency both as a characteristic of giftedness and as an intellectual skill to be developed. In the USA, Paul Torrance (1962) has been particularly influential in demonstrating the role of these factors in education. What he advocates is as relevant for children with special needs and the generality of children as it is for the gifted, particularly as he recognizes the importance of developing thinking abilities within the context of the curriculum. We summarize below the strategies he advocates:

1. Creativity as intrinsic or self-motivation
2. Facilitating creativity
   - Incompleteness and openness
     - strategies usually effective *before* a learning activity
     - strategies usually effective *during* a learning activity
     - strategies usually effective *following* a learning activity
   - Making something and then doing something with it
   - Stimulating pupils to question and to ask questions

The sensitive parent or teacher will immediately recognize that while these suggestions may be stimulating and provide opportunities for enlivening learning and stimulating involvement and curiosity, the purpose and relevance to the learner must not be lost sight of. As Bruner (1960) reminds us, 'the value of any piece of learning, over and above the enjoyment it gives, is that it should be relevant to us in the future'. With keen, bright young children, their curiosity and eagerness to master new skills may need little stimulation if they can see the relevance of what they are required to do. For all children need to see pattern and structure in what they are learning, whether it be a skill or an intellectual task. True creativity can only operate when children have mastered all that is known about a subject and when they have mastered the skills or methods appropriate to it. In his essay on the aims of education, Alfred North Whitehead (1929), the distinguished mathematician and philosopher who collaborated with Russell on the *Principia Mathematica*, said of the child's mind between the ages of 8 and 13, 'It is dominated by wonder, and cursed be the dullard who destroys wonder.' The art of instruction is to keep wonder alive while facilitating the acquisition of skills and knowledge. As Whitehead also wrote: 'Education must essentially be a setting in order of a ferment already stirring in the mind.'

Increasing Creativity and Problem Solving

Polya (1971) hoped that his classic work *How to Solve It* would 'open up a vista of mental activity on the highest level' and, by demonstrating how mathematical method may be used to solve problems, he has performed an invaluable service for generations of researchers. His method, extended in his later books on induction and analogy and on plausible inference, has a scientific, mathematical basis. In discussing heuristic reasoning, for example, he stresses that the

> . . . reasoning is reasoning not regarded as final and strict but as provisional and plausible only, whose purpose is to discover the solution of the present problem . . . Heuristic reasoning is good in itself. What is bad is to mix up heuristic reasoning with rigorous proof. What is worse is to sell heuristic reasoning for rigorous proof.

Unfortunately, much of what has been suggested by many psychologists and educators for improving creativity and problem solving is not susceptible of proof. When their proposals are supported by anecdote and descriptions of their methods we can, at least, try them and test their efficacy. When it is suggested that they are effective because they tap into our right hemisphere or temporal lobes, we may wish for more rigorous proof and wonder how we ever managed without them. What evidence there is for neurological localization does not account for the observable differences in the performance of individuals. As with all skills and abilities, some people have natural aptitudes which with training enable them to perform exceptionally well; others have little aptitude, received no or little training and perform exceptionally badly. What we can do is to help all children to perform better and the methods described in this section may benefit some of them.

Sidney Parnes (1976) developed ideas which were first tried out 40 years earlier by Alex Osborn and described in his *Applied Imagination* (1963). Osborn's use of brainstorming as a way of producing ideas to help solve problems reminds us of the stress placed by many investigators on the fluency of ideas which characterizes creative thinkers.

1. *Fact finding*: assembling all the information available relevant to the problem.
2. *Problem finding*: the obvious first step is defining and stating the problem and thoroughly understanding it and all the factors involved. As in previous methods we have discussed, a period is allowed for participants to stand aside from the problem. A day, during which the problem is ignored, is customarily recommended for incubation.
3. *Idea finding – brainstorming*: this is the method used for generating ideas which has had more currency in advertising than in academic situations. Sitting in circles with no more than half a dozen in each group is recommended in order to encourage maximum participation. The participants are encouraged to throw out ideas and to defer judgement about them. Unlikely suggestions are encouraged and free-wheeling, as it is called, is welcomed, as it demonstrates flexible thinking. Pace is important and the more ideas produced the better the session is thought to be going. Hitch-hiking or piggybacking is also encouraged: taking up other people's ideas and developing them or using them to start a new line of suggestions. Pupils usually find 5–10 minutes of brainstorming is enough, but Parnes originally recommend 45-minute sessions. Complex problems are best broken down into parts which can be dealt with in the time allowed. The groups record their ideas and, at each break, share their most potent suggestions. Psychologically, brainstorming is a form of free association, but its use in this context derives from the stress placed on divergent thinking.
4. *Solution finding*: the participants now review the ideas generated and, having identified those which appear most feasible, evaluate them according to the way in which they fit the problem's criteria until a possible solution is found.

5. *Acceptance finding*: this is the final stage at which a check back is made to see that the solution fits and that it meets all the criteria.

Parker (1989) has developed a more curriculum-related form of problem solving as part of her Leadership Training Model. The model incorporates ideas from Dewey, Torrance and Wallas with those of the above Osborn/Parnes model:

1. Problem perception and definition
2. Incubation
3. Creative thinking brainstorming
4. Analysis
5. Evaluation
6. Implementation

Synectics

A method of problem solving and facilitating inventiveness developed by Gordon (1961), synectics is similar to Polya's approach in its use of analogies: direct, personal, symbolic and fantasy analogies. An example of *direct analogy* is Leonardo da Vinci's attempt to build a flying machine in which a man operates wings like those of a bird, or Gutenberg seeing the solution to his printing problem in the wine-press. *Personal analogy* is imagining what one would do in a situation, such as scaring away birds by making a scarecrow or trying to anticipate what tactics one's opponent might adopt by imagining oneself in his position. *Symbolic analogy* uses symbolism to solve problems, as in the case of the Montgolfier brothers who, realizing that smoke and gas rise, invented the hot-air balloon. *Fantasy analogy* is the application of Freudian wish-fulfilment: 'In our wildest dreams, how would we like this problem solved or this invention to work?' This is like the 'if only' imaginative thinking we spoke about earlier, as, for example, designing a house for an earthquake zone after wishing it could rise and fall like a ship on a stormy sea.

Creative thinking, brainstorming, problem solving and synectic group methods of invention are interesting in the light they throw on how people think gifted people solve problems and are themselves examples of Gordon's 'personal analogy'. They only work when those using them have mastered all the facts and have tried out their solutions. In the real world, pure science can stream ahead of applied science, as in the case of space research, which often lags behind until suitable materials have been developed to make the application of theories practicable. The analogy of a firework rocket travelling on into space took years to implement. Man has long seen the potential in harnessing the power of storms, but we have a long way to go before we can do so. Pupils who are in the process of learning a subject have so much to learn that it is quite unrealistic to expect them to learn by the discovery method and start in term 1 with reinventing the wheel and finish in term 30 with building a nuclear fusion plant. But we can familiarize them by giving them guided exploratory activities, so that they learn the methodology of their subjects.

One curriculum model which addresses this problem of educating gifted children in inquiry and problem-solving skills is Renzulli's (1977) Enrichment Triad Model. This introduces subjects in a way which encourages guided exploration, identifies problems and trains pupils in the appropriate research methods by which to study them. Pupils will also be greatly helped if they learn something of the lives and the thinking of those who have contributed to the knowledge they need to acquire. They may then learn that what helped Henri Poincaré to know he had found the right solutions to his problems was 'the feeling of mathematical beauty, of the harmony of number, of forms, of geometric elegance. This is a true aesthetic feeling that all mathematicians know.' They will know, too, that he was not alone and that Jacques Hadamard (1949) wrote in his study of distinguished American mathematicians' methods of working: 'The sense of beauty as a "drive" for discovery in our mathematical field, seems to be almost the only one.'

For, in all of this understandable desire to develop creativity, to develop verbal and ideational fluency, there is a central problem which many creative and intellectually gifted people would find uncongenial. For many mathematicians, architects, engineers, writers, poets, musicians, artists and athletes, their thinking is done outside words and language in vague, trance-like feelings, in barely perceived images and half understood visions. Just as some need silence and others music as a white noise to remove them from the immediacy of their surroundings or as a force to lift them above the sometimes unavoidably repetitive ritual of their craft, adolescents may need to feel anchored to their peer-group music while they study. As Einstein wrote to Hadamard:

> The words or the language, as they are written or spoken, do not seem to play any role in my mechanism of thought. The physical entities which seem to serve as elements in thought are certain signs and more or less clear images which can be 'voluntarily' reproduced and combined.

This is not to deny the value and importance of language for the communication of thought, but it is to suggest that in creativity, when we wish to go beyond the known, beyond the given, the precision of language may prevent us taking the cognitive leap or seeing the vague images or patterns of the new and unknown. Then, when the mind sees, language in turn must be transformed. Faraday saw the lines of force as fields around his magnets and the word field thereafter took on new meaning.

Many teachers have found that, once they have aroused children's interest in a subject, it helps if the children close their eyes and wait for the words and images to float up to the surface of their minds before starting to write. Wordsworth succinctly described the phenomenon: 'Poetry is the spontaneous overflow of powerful feelings: it takes its origin from emotion recollected in tranquillity.'

Finally, one of the problems of teaching problem solving and creative thinking is that one is very much in danger of teaching 'dry swimming': exercising a skill out of its proper environment. If we want children to solve problems, learn to investigate and research, we must first provide them with the knowledge of the subjects in which those skills are exercised. Solving problems of double stopping or harmony in music are different from solving problems in topology or chemistry. Children need to know what to think about and what facts, ideas or factors it is appropriate to think with. This implies that we should teach them in the cognitive style of the subject. If we believe mathematics is aesthetically beautiful, we must demonstrate this characteristic. In the majority of cases, we will teach in the exploratory mode, guiding learners into the most useful, significant areas, giving them insights into the concepts and thought amplifiers, the taxonomies and key ideas to which we have the map and know its scales and legends. Above all, we will want them to feel that we are enthusiastic about the route we are taking them down and still able to share with them the excitement of unravelling the problems it poses. It has been said that only when we have adopted the values and methods of a subject and made them our own can we be said to be on the way to its mastery: we have studied pottery and wish to become a potter or have studied veterinary surgery and wish to become a vet. In the words of Yehudi Menuhin (1977), 'Perfection cannot be achieved unless its pursuit becomes a way of life.' If gifted children pursue excellence in the subject or subjects of their choice, we may be confident that in the process they will develop the skills and the appetite to be creative in it.

'The Woman Question'

Whatever differences there are between male and female neonates, nurture and education will make them more different. Women are different from men genetically – being saved the complication of the Y chromosome – and hormonally and, clearly, social factors affect the development and status of women. This applies to all women, whether or not they are gifted. Enough has been written about sex-typing and the inequality of women without the necessity for us to examine the subject here. Suffice it to say that, from Galton (1869) onwards, with some few exceptions, genius has been seen as eminence and men as more eminent than women. It was maintained by Le Bon, (1879) that women had smaller brains, were physically weaker and were intellectually inferior to men. Such research evidence from a founder of social psychology, supporting patriarchy, confirmed women's role as Kinder-Küche-Kirche.

It was a view challenged by Leta Hollingworth (Silverman, 1989), herself a gifted child, born in Nebraska in 1886, whose mother died when she was 3 years old and whose education began in a one-room schoolhouse where 'We had small classes (twelve pupils, in all), all nature for a laboratory, and individualized instruction.' As a young married woman graduate, she found herself denied both a teaching post in New York State and a fellowship to study in Columbia University. Frustrated by a life of domestic chores, she determined to attack the problem of the predicament of women in a similar position to her own. In 1913, she took an MA degree in education. Her thesis on 'Functional Periodicity' demonstrated that, throughout their menstrual cycle, women were as productive as men and that there was no justification, on the grounds of their periodicity, for refusing to employ women.

Throughout her distinguished career as a researcher, psychologist and educationist, she continued to address the problems of women and the myths of their inferiority. The commonly held view at the time was that not only were women inferior to men but variations between women were less than variations between men. First, she attacked this variability hypothesis by showing that there were as many mentally defective girls as there were defective boys. Boys were referred for classification because it was feared that they would never contribute to the family or be able to support themselves; girls were not referred but were kept at home to do the chores. She next attacked Galton's notion that superior mental ability and eminence were identical, pointing out that 'education and opportunity are the prime determinants of achievement, since nearly all the great men have been born in comfortable homes, of parents in superior circumstances'. Thus, she argued, the small number of eminent women was due to sociological limitations rather than biological factors.

Hollingworth also made an analysis of Terman's research and found that girls scored two or three points higher than boys for all age groups up to age 14 on the standardized Stanford-Binet scores and that the highest scorers in Terman's longitudinal study were attained by girls with IQs of 190 plus. Again, she argued that it was environmental factors that limited the number of eminent women. In her own studies of giftedness, begun in 1916, Hollingworth, unlike Terman, was concerned with the influence of environment, particularly education, upon achievement. It is this work (Hollingworth, 1942), written up by her husband after her death, that is frequently quoted. She repeatedly emphasized the vital importance of the first 12 years. At a time when gifted children were accelerated through the grades, she found that children with IQs over 140 wasted half their time in school and those over 170 wasted most of the time. Instead of acceleration, she advocated the homogeneous grouping of gifted pupils in the 7–13 age group with a curriculum centred around their interests. One of her major contributions was the devising of the curricula for an experimental school for slow learners and gifted pupils. The curriculum for the latter emphasized initiative, originality, creativity and independent study, combined with the teaching of major principles. She considered the recognition, education, realization and utilization of gifted pupils 'one of the most important of all problems for the development of social science'. She summed up the problem of gifted women as:

> Stated briefly, 'the woman question' is how to reproduce the species and at the same time to work, and to realize work's full reward, in accordance with individual ability.

It would be naive to believe that the question has been fully answered. Children begin learning sex roles – both their own and those of the opposite sex – at around 2 or 3 years of age, as shown in their play (Piaget, 1951). Despite changes in attitudes to sex roles in society, Kaye (1982) found that, in a representative sample of families, at least 90 per cent of young infants spent 90 per cent of their waking hours with their mothers, and the rest with grandmothers, aunts or female neighbours. Not surprisingly, therefore, children develop social perceptions of their gender identity and sex roles from these familial and social interactions irrespective of their genetic sex in these early years.

Over the years, attempts have been made to identify gender differences in intellectual functioning (Maccoby and Jacklin, 1974) and to relate these to differences of brain hemispheric structure and localization or to hormones. Much of the research is reviewed by Rose *et al.* (1984), who conclude that such gender differences as do exist are modified in the plastic, adaptive brains of infants by social influences irrespective of genetic sex: 'Psychocultural expectations profoundly shape a person's gender development in ways which do not reduce to body chemistry.' Increasingly, as women themselves play a greater role in the sciences, they are re-examining the evidence and making their own contributions to this subject (Merchant, 1980).

Reis and Callahan (1989) address themselves to the question, 'Gifted females: They've come a long way – or have they?', and point out that more attention has been given to issues relating to the potential and achievements of gifted females in the last 5 years than in the previous five decades. Not all of this interest has been of value: often minute sex differences in cognitive functioning have been translated into categorical assumptions about individuals 'which belie the broad variation within each sex'. They, too, like Hollingworth, find that 'equal ability and achievement do not guarantee equal opportunity to achieve success and satisfaction with career choice', and cited the following as fact in 1989: (1) although females receive higher grades than males throughout their academic lives, only 2 per cent of US patentees were women; (2) there were only two females in the US Senate, only one female cabinet member and women made up only 5 per cent of the members of the House of Representatives; (3) women owned only 7 per cent of US businesses, only 10 per cent of full professors were women and not one woman occupied a leading position in the top five US orchestras; (4) women college graduates employed full-time earned, on average, the same as a man with only a high school diploma. But, they point out, it may be necessary to re-examine the concept of under-achievement by adult women and the choices they make about their careers and having a family from the standpoint of sex and gender differences, if such differences exist.

Among other things, Reis and Callahan have surveyed the meta-analyses of studies relating to the psychology of gender by Hyde and Linn (1986), Becker (1986) and Whitley *et al.* (1986), and conclude with Chipman (1988) that in view of the infrequency with which differences are identified, the relative lack of their predictability and the smallness of such differences, that research needs to be reoriented. They recommend that research is needed to address factors mediating gender differences in achievements and environmental variables which may be manipulated to ensure that the development of females is not inhibited and choices are not foreclosed. Like Hollingworth, they urge closer examination of the differences within girls to find 'those characteristics likely to be influenced by the environment and those experiences and conditions conducive to full development potential'.

Rather than compare, for example, the performance of girls and boys in mathematics, they suggest that it is more useful to examine internal comparisons made by girls as they engage in decision making about maths and science courses and careers. Eccles (1987) identifies the following conditions which distinguish teachers who have been successful in keeping females interested in those subjects:

- Frequent use of cooperative learning.
- Frequent individualized learning.
- Frequent hands-on opportunities.
- Use of practical problems in assignments.
- Active career and educational guidance.

- Infrequent competitive motivational strategies.
- Frequent activities to broaden views of maths and the physical sciences
  – presenting maths as a tool in solving problems.
- Frequent full-class participation.

Other factors identified by Eccles include: the significance of social stereotypes; the assumption that it is innate ability not work which results in achievement; parental attitudes that regard maths as being more difficult for girls than for boys and less important than English, even when the girls are scoring top marks in both subjects or are outperforming the boys; girls perceive success in traditionally female careers as due to ability, whereas success in stereotypically male careers is considered as the result of hard work and luck.

The attitudes of teachers clearly influence girls and Sadker and Sadker (1985) found that, in the classrooms of more than 100 fourth-, fifth- and sixth-grade classes in four states and the District of Columbia, in all subjects boys dominated classroom communication and that 'High achieving girls received the least attention.' Arnold and Denny (1985), in their longitudinal studies of high academic achievers, found that girls underestimated their abilities after leaving high school and entering college and lowered their career aspirations. Reis (in press) found that counselling, giving positive role models and highlighting female accomplishments could counteract this and increase enrolment in advanced mathematics and science courses. They also cite the evidence of Fox (1977) and Lee and Bryk (1986), which indicates that girls may do best in preponderantly female classes, taught by women in single-sex schools, and argue that the implications of these findings on the achievement of gifted girls has still to be explored.

Reis and Callahan conclude by emphasizing the importance of avoiding categorization and stereotypes and of research which is founded on an understanding of the processes of learning and development. What they do not address – it being outside their immediate concern – is the importance for women of not only academic and career success but also of their self-realization as women. This was at the heart of Hollingworth's posing of 'the woman question': how to reproduce the species, work, enjoy the rewards of work and realize one's intellectual potential. As she recognized: 'This is a question primarily of the gifted, for the discontent with and resentment against women's work have originated chiefly among women exceptionally well endowed with intellect.'

Many of the stereotypes have already disappeared. Some mothers earn more than fathers, more women are beginning to penetrate male preserves in medicine, engineering, politics, the law and national security, more women are working, more have their own businesses or are in positions of authority. That much more needs to be done is not in dispute. This is underlined when we contrast the above US research with Freeman's (1991) longitudinal study. She found that 30 per cent of boys compared with 5 per cent of girls found their greatest satisfaction in achievement; 93 per cent of those who saw themselves as achievers were boys, whereas 73 per cent of those who saw themselves as creatives were girls; boys attributed success to ability and hard work, girls looked upon it as something outside their control (e.g. luck) but regarded lack of success as their own fault. Girls saw success as a threat to their femininity and tended to work best in single-sex schools which were preferred by most of their parents. At GCE, girls passed more subjects but, at A levels or Highers, boys gained twice as many A grades as girls. More boys went to university with more girls going to colleges and polytechnics, and both the girls and their parents seemed to accept a lower intellectual form of higher education for daughters than for sons, despite 'parents' pro-testations about equal aims for sons and daughters'. All of the girls who went to university had been at an all-girls school for most of their lives, and all of the boys who entered university from a comprehensive school had studied science. As Freeman acknowledges, this is in line with evidence from much larger studies.

The influence of parents' opinions and sex roles comes out clearly in Freeman's study: science for boys, arts for girls. Three times as many boys as girls specialized in science; over twice as many girls as boys specialized in the arts; five girls went on to study music, whereas no boys did. As the girls got older, the chances of them being taught science by a woman fell from 56 per cent at 10 years of age to 14 per cent at A level physics. The gifted pupils in her sample were those most likely to have attended a single-sex school – as the highly academic schools for which they were selected tended to be single-sex schools – yet only 14.2 per cent of the sample would have chosen a single-sex education. Most of these girls felt they would have been at a disadvantage with boys in the class. Both the boys and girls commented on the fact that single-sex schools failed to prepare them 'for the social aspects of growing up'. Some of the girls found that 'they were not always made to feel at home' in some prestigious, academic boys' schools, which admitted very bright girls into their sixth forms. She concludes: 'In the last decades of the twentieth century, then, the forces of prescribed gender roles were still seen to be moulding the lives of these gifted girls and boys.' Reading her comments about some schools which she describes as 'decidedly Victorian' is indeed worrying.

In planning educational provisions for exceptionally able and gifted girls, we need to look at the curriculum and school organization in the ways that these researchers have indicated and in the context of ensuring that the motivational, emotional, social and cultural components of their developing and changing personalities are also considered. Only this will ensure that they have the opportunity to exercise choice in the ways in which they grow as people. And, once again, we must recognize that this is what we would want for all women, however intellectually endowed. What genetics tells us is that there are no stereotypes, we are each unique. There is no biochemical predeterminism. As Dr Steve Jones concluded one of his Reith Lectures in 1991, 'although genetics may tell us a lot about where we come from, it says nothing about what we are'.

What we are is a result of the interaction of where we come from with that equally unpredetermined mix of environmental factors. While no hard evidence exists of sex differences in brain organization being related to sex differences in intellectual abilities, there is no doubt that tertiary sexual characteristics (Brown, 1987) are determined by socio-physiological forces, by family, peer group, economic and other social influences such as the media. Education is one of the social forces we can control. In the light of the foregoing researches, we need to control it much more sensitively and wisely to develop the abilities and enhance the lives of women.

The contributions of outstanding women such as Byron's daughter, Ada Augusta, Countess of Lovelace, a brilliant mathematician whose description of Charles Babbage's mechanical computer preserved the knowledge of it for future generations, of Marie Curie and Dorothy C. Hodgkin, both of whom won the Nobel prize for chemistry, of writers such as Jane Austen, the Brontës and George Eliot, or the leadership of Catherine the Great and Elizabeth I are significant because of their rarity. If we search the lists of Nobel prize winners or of the members of America's Hall of Fame we will have difficulty in finding the names of a score of women among the many hundreds of men. If we try to name a dozen women composers or artists of international repute, most of us will have difficulties. It is as if society has failed to develop half its human potential until we recall that, if 90 per cent of children spend 90 per cent of their time with women, at any one time a lot of women are busy with infants. We should also recognize that at any one time very few women are killing anyone or, for that matter, have ever been directly engaged in mass slaughter unlike the male of their species.

In striving for equality, it is important that, now that women in much of the developed world can decide whether or not they have children and when they wish to have them, factors which have already changed their tertiary sexual characteristics, they should be actively involved in writing the agenda for educational and social provisions which will help them to realize their potential without sacrificing or contaminating those attributes and abilities which have contributed to the survival of the species and to the more life-enhancing aspects of civilization. Tokenism and obstructions to their liberation from all the complex trappings of patriarchal society need to be recognized and removed. Every curriculum, and not least the hidden curricula of our schools, colleges, universities and teaching hospitals, therefore, need careful scrutiny.

CHAPTER 7

Extraordinary People and Prodigies

The Savant Syndrome

Keith's hands and legs twitch and twist. His head writhes as he tries to speak.

'When is your birthday?' he asks, forcing the words out through the jaw and lips which go into spasm whenever he wants to use them. I tell him the date.

'How old are you?' Keith likes this question. Adults always look taken aback by it. He's spluttering with laughter. I admit my age.

'Thursday,' he tells me straight away. 'You were born on a Thursday.'

'That's right. That's what you told me last time I was here.' My response momentarily nonplusses him. His head jerks round and up and he stares at me. His eyes smile.

'Tuesday, seventeenth May, last year,' he splutters. He is right, of course.

'What's new, Keith?'

His hand swoops at the keyboard. The screen scrolls and halts at a spread-sheet of the school timetable for next term. He looks proudly up at me. He'd worked it out in a fraction of the time it would have taken the head. Keith had been transformed from the handicapped boy with the birthday calendar trick into a valuable member of the school community. Giving him a function in which his gift could be used had not only given him status, it had extended his ability into a new area and given another indicator of how his abilities might be developed to give him greater control over himself and his environment.

There are many pupils with special educational needs who, like Keith, have islands of extraordinary ability in mathematics, music, art, athletics, literature or courage. Stephen Wiltshire's drawings of London, Venice and Moscow delight us not merely by their dextrous draughtsmanship but because they at once absorb and reveal something of the mind of a young man whose thoughts would otherwise be inaccessible to us. We marvel, too, at how it is possible for someone to draw what he has seen with such accurate perspective when it took artists centuries before they invented its rules. Can it be that his clenched hand is tracing with such delicacy the images his mind projects upon the paper?

Perhaps the most remarkable child we have encountered was Mervin, who at 8 years of age had no speech and was constantly and violently active, careering around the assessment centre without discernible pause and oblivious to everything said to him like a wild creature in a cage. He had a small repertoire of behaviours, all of them bizarre, such as leaping at people and clinging to them or sweeping everything off other children's tables. Physical, psychological and neurological tests had been unable to determine what could be done to help Mervin. He could walk and run and feed himself, and his caring and exhausted parents had succeeded in training him to be continent. Thanks to them he had been assessed as having the developmental age of a 3-year-old. In the course of planning to introduce some behaviour modification which she thought might help Mervin, his teacher had begun by attempting to observe his attention span as he hurtled from place to place about the unit. He paused longest at a particular desk on which was an open book. It was then that she discovered that Mervin could read. Further careful investigation revealed that he could read at the 8-year-old level. With no ascertainable intelligence and no known instruction, somehow, while in a state of perpetual motion, Mervin had taught himself to read. Reading at his chronological level with a developmental age of 3 would suggest a mental ability quotient of over 250!

Darold A. Treffert (1990), the US psychiatrist, has described what he calls 'extraordinary people' in medical history, with many of whom he has had personal experience. Dr Langdon Down, who identified Down's Syndrome, also coined the term 'idiot savant'. Appropriately, Treffert describes their condition as Savant Syndrome, which he defines as a condition in which someone with major mental illness or major intellectual handicap has spectacular islands of ability and brilliance in stark contrast to those handicaps. Some he terms talented savants, in that their skills are remarkable in contrast to their disabilities; others are those rare prodigious savants whose skills would be remarkable even if present in normals.

The many cases he discusses include blind, autistic, hydro- and micro-encephalic, mentally retarded, epileptic, cerebral palsied, and retrolental fibroplasic patients whose blindness may have been the result of excessive oxygen administered to them as premature babies. The skills that they demonstrated included drawing, musical, mnemonic, mathematical, engineering and sculptural abilities. Treffert examines the various theories and hypotheses, such as eidetic imagery, put forward over the decades to account for the phenomenon, and reviews the literature of the researches carried out by autopsy, psychiatrists, CAT scans and C-EEG. What concerns us here, however, is the conclusions he comes to about the upbringing and education of these savants.

Parents and professionals directly involved with extraordinary people are rightly concerned about the dangers of exploitation, of parading them before the press and cameras to perform like circus animals for cash. He is refreshingly sensible in his approach to this problem, pointing out that 'having a savant use his or her special skills and abilities, whether in the living room, on the hospital unit, on stage or before a camera, if he or she is willing to do so, is not exploitation'. The difficulty is, of course, how one determines whether or not the savants are willing and fully understand what is happening. Not only is considerable sensitivity necessary, but it has to be said that if the interests of the savants are not paramount and are subsidiary to the interests of someone else, then exploitation will take place, whether for money or self-interest. That stricture is equally applicable to researchers: no research should take place unless safeguards are built in to ensure that the savant benefits from the experience. What concerns Treffert is clearly the happiness of his patients. In so far as one can be confident that parents, carers, professionals and others involved with the savants, appreciate their special skillls as but one part of their uniqueness, and that the savants 'love to use their skills, just as the rest of us do, to gain a sense of achievement, pride and satisfaction', it is reasonable to agree with him.

What emerges from his detailed and close studies of cases such as Leslie Lemke, who was born blind and with cerebral palsy, is that savants can learn and continue to make progress in their skills and can also develop other competencies through the exercise of their skills. Leslie had both eyes removed before he was 6 months old when he was adopted by May Lemke who was aged 52. A neurologist later diagnosed spastic paraplegia and echolalia. By the age of 5½ years, May had taught him to walk and he could speak, repeating verbatim and mimicking all the conversations he had heard during the day. By 7 years, like May, he could play the piano by ear; by 8 he could play other instruments, including the ukelele, concertina, xylophone and accordion. At 10½ years of age, he was still found to have no conversation and to be largely repetitive and imitative. He could not dress himself or use a knife and fork.

By the age of 12, he was playing and singing competently and at 14, having heard it once on television, played the theme music of a film,

Tchaikovsky's Piano Concerto No. 1, without mistake from beginning to end. He has subsequently appeared on a number of television programmes and regularly gives concerts. He has a prodigious memory, can transpose an opera he has heard to the piano whilst singing the parts in the foreign language in which he heard them, can accompany singers, play duets and improvise. His repertoire ranges from hymns to Greig and Gershwin. When May developed Alzheimer's disease, her daughter, Mary, took over the care of Leslie. His speech has continued to improve and he can now feed himself. His musical abilities have extended to composition. At the age of 34, Leslie was given a complete neurological and neuropsychological examination and found to function at the moderately retarded level of intelligence, verbal reasoning was in the moderately to severely retarded range (WAIS-R Verbal Quotient 58) and non-verbal reasoning skills were in the severely retarded range. A CAT scan showed left-sided abnormality, especially in the area of the left eye socket and the left frontal lobe. He was diagnosed as having atonic diplegia, scoliosis and his left lower leg was 4 cm shorter than his right lower leg. But this blind musician regularly performs a rigorous concert schedule in America and around the world and he had recently completed a tour of 26 cities in Japan. He continues to grow as a musician and as a person. His enjoyment of his gift and of the applause it earns him are apparent to all who hear him.

Treffert, from his studies of this and many similar cases, is convinced that constant care, understanding, acceptance, high expectations, support and encouragement combined with a fostering of whatever talents a person may have is special education at its finest. He cites the work of Hope University, UNICO National College, Anaheim, California, the only fine arts college in the world established specifically for the gifted mentally retarded. Its major sponsoring charity is the UNICO National, an Italian-American service organization.

> A student's talent is used to draw him or her out and serve as a pathway to more function, more independence and more self-worth. The school philosophy stresses 'whole person' development and the performing groups 'allow the students to showcase their talents and, in addition to entertaining their audiences, prove that there are hidden talents among our handicapped citizens that need to be discovered, trained and nurtured'.

His advice can best be summed up, in his own words, as minimizing deficits and maximizing strengths, while using the savant's skills as 'a window to the world for the savant, and . . . as a window to the savant for the rest of us. Training the talent can diminish the defect.' What must delight Stephen Wiltshire's family and friends is the way in which his language and communication skills have grown with his talent and diminished his disability. Hearing him talk in a television programme about Dustin Hoffman's portrayal of a savant in the film *Rain Man*, to which Darold Treffert was a consultant, also shows what insight he has gained into himself.

Whether the savants are autistic, blind or deaf, spastic or ataxic, the message is the same, the syndrome is a regularly recurring cluster of symptoms and traits from which we can learn to help them to realize more of themselves and from which we may learn more about ourselves, about memory, skills and abilities, creativity and intellect. It is important that, in considering gifted children, we recognize, too, the needs of these children with islands of ability in a sea of silence or who are locked in the mocking cages of bodies they can scarcely control. We should also have particular concern for the needs of their parents, carers and teachers whose patience and ingenuity, and whose love or 'unconditional positive regard', are vital to them.

'What Prodigies Surprise'

Aged 10, Carol went to grammar school as an under-age pupil. During her first week she accidentally tripped over a senior prefect's foot. She upbraided him roundly and was duly reported to her house mistress who, being sympathetic, gave her a gentle admonishment and the task of writing an essay on 'Why Prefects Should be Shown Respect'. Carol handed in her essay which, the house mistress had to admit, was as brilliantly a succinct philosophical demolition of the prefectoral system as any sixth-former could have written.

Toby, aged 10, had been brought to see the educational psychologist because his parents thought his school was not extending him sufficiently. While the psychologist discussed this with his parents, Toby had been invited to choose a book to read from the educational psychologist's bookcase. Later, when the psychologist called Toby into his room, he asked him what he'd been reading.

'Oh, it was only a book about differential calculus', he said. 'By the way, there's a misprint in the equation at the beginning of Chapter 4.'

Prodigies are too often thought of as precocious child musicians or as precocious chess players such as Gata Kamsky who, at 16, shared first place in the Interpolis Chess Tournament in 1990. In our experience, they are encountered in most large schools and they may show their talents in games, athletics, music, ballet, chess, arts and crafts, horticulture, the subjects of the curriculum or any other human activity of cultural significance. It is one of the values of Radford's (1990) comprehensive study of child prodigies and exceptional children that it is not limited to those who have excelled in academic subjects or the arts but embraces outstanding young achievers in sports, athletics, business, entertainment, bravery, altruism and spirituality.

Musicians

Prodigies are most apparent in music and mathematics because they are solitary activities which are not limited by the need to be literate or dependent upon physical maturity, and are unencumbered by the restrictions of schools. Early parental identification and influence, whether around the gypsy campfire, family piano or radio respectively, got Django Reinhardt, Solomon and Jacqueline du Pré off to an early start. Mozart, the classic prodigy, was taught by his father, began the harpsichord at age 3, composed at 5, when he performed in public, and filled the rest of his 35 years with music-making and composing. Where a parent is not the initial inspirator and teacher, it is common for musical and other prodigies to identify with a tutor or mentor. Mendelssohn, who was perhaps as talented as Mozart, gave his first piano recital aged 9, was tutored in composition by Goethe's friend, Zelter, under whom he made remarkable progress and from whom he took over the championship of Bach's music, which had by that time fallen into neglect.

Menuhin (1977) relates in his autobiography how, as a result of his frequent attendance at concerts at the Curran Theatre in San Francisco, he identified, before he was 4, the violin as the instrument he wished to learn to play and Louis Persinger as the man he wanted to teach him. Later, aged 10, on his first visit to Europe, he persuaded Enesco, 'the supreme master', to teach him. Jacqueline du Pré's love of music was undoubtedly initiated by her mother, a gifted pianist who had won a scholarship to the London School of Dalcroze Eurythmics when she was 18. By the time she was 4, Jacqueline could play pieces on the piano simply from listening to her older sister's lessons. However, it was just before her fifth birthday that she heard a *Children's Hour* programme on BBC Radio about the instruments of the orchestra and heard a cello. 'I fell in love with it straightaway. Something within the instrument spoke to me, and it's been my friend ever since.'

Musical prodigies, whether composers such as Mozart or performers like Rubinstein, have a natural advantage over the generality of the population in that they develop the neuromuscular dexterities, sensory discrimination and musical sensibilities when they are young. Whatever propensities or predispositions they may have, such as musical memory or perfect pitch, they are able to accept and to enjoy the practice which is essential for the achievement of mastery. Their abilities are asserted and become, with recognition and encouragement, almost obsessive. Menuhin broke the toy violin he was given as a present because he couldn't stand the sound it made.

There are very few great musicians, whether performers or composers, who have not demonstrated their abilities and interest early in their lives, often singing before they talked, but we have no means of knowing how many more great musicians might have developed had their abilities been recognized and developed. Musical parents may well recognize early giftedness, but musical giftedness does not occur only in musical families. Musical children born into homes in which the TV and transistor are aural wallpaper may find the noise excruciating. Perhaps only in church, club or school is there a chance that they will experience pleasure from music and their abilities be recognized. Louis Armstrong's musical ability was manifest when he sang on the streets of New Orleans in a boys' quartet but he learned the trumpet when he was 13, in the Coloured Waifs' Home where he was taught by Peter Davis; later his mentor was Joe Oliver. Without musical teachers, as opposed to teachers of music who are unqualified and teach behind the Chinese Wall of an upright piano, the chances of them being discovered in school are remote indeed. Local Education Authorities (LEAs) which attempt to staff all schools with qualified music teachers – a virtual impossibility – provide a corps of qualified instrumental teachers and foster orchestras and festivals, have no difficulty in finding talented pupils, but they may have difficulty in finding instruments for them. Where this isn't done, many parents may find the burden of the cost of lessons, instruments and travelling beyond them.

Mathematicians

Mathematicians, as we have seen, are frequently first taught or encouraged by their parents. John Adams, of Asfordby, Leicestershire, read at the age of 2, used a computer at 3 and at the age of 8 passed O level at grade B helped by his father and mother with half-an-hour's nightly 'homework'. At 9, he passed A level at grade C. Ganesh Sittampalam of Surbiton, gained A level at grade A when 9 and at Surrey University in 1992, aged 13, a first-class honours maths degree, Britain's youngest graduate. Like John Adams and Ruth Lawrence, who started her maths degree course at Oxford, aged 12, he was first taught by his father. But arithmetical calculations can be performed in the head and survive intact when parents are unresponsive, as Gauss's father appears to have been. Einstein showed no early promise at school, save in mathematics, and at college cut lectures, preferring to read theoretical physics.

Writers

Precocity in poetry and literature is less common, requiring wide reading and familiarity with form and style. But children who have read widely may well start writing when they are 9 or 10. Daisy Ashford's *The Young Visiters* was written when she was 9 years old. This short popular romance is attractive because of its unwitting naivety. Feldman (1986) cites the case of a boy who taught himself to type at 3 and who by 14 was writing lyrics for rock music.

We have been particularly impressed, however, with the ability of some young children to express in writing deep and often mature and disturbing feelings. One 10-year-old, Lynn, captain of her school netball team, when her class had been encouraged to write verse for the school magazine, handed in an exercise-book of her own poetry which would have been considered mature in both form and content had it been written by an adolescent. Another 10-year-old, Desmond whom we described earlier, whose mother had died and whose father was dying, was almost mute and antisocial with loss and anger but expressed himself in vitriolic poetry with an intensty of language which brought to mind John Donne's or Francis Thompson's imagery, save that he was pouring his scorn upon the faith that they held dear. Thomas Chatterton had his first poem published in 1762, when he was 10, and had filled a number of notebooks with his writings before he was 12.

But it is usually in adolescence that prodigies reveal themselves in writing. Arthur Rimbaud, after being a model schoolboy, ran away to Paris at the age of 15, and immersed himself in occult writing in his determination to become a poetic visionary. His profound influence on French literature was the result of the poetry and prose poems he wrote before the age of 20. Dylan Thomas began writing poetry while still at school and his first book of poetry was published when he was 20. David Gascoyne's first volume of poetry was published when he was 16 but, more remarkably, he was only 19 when his *A Short Survey of Surrealism* was published in 1935, a year before the International Surrealist Exhibition. In the USA, John Kennedy Toole's comic masterpiece *A Confederacy of Dunces* was published posthumously (1980), as the result of his mother's efforts after he, like Chatterton, committed suicide, aged 31, when he failed to get it published and fame had eluded him. Toole, who was talented academically as well as musically and artistically, had been accelerated at school, skipping two grammar school grades and gaining scholarships to college and university. His earlier novel, *The Neon Bible* (1990), was written when he was 16, and is remarkable for its portrayal of childhood loneliness in an atmosphere of religious bigotry and small-town small-mindedness.

Artists

> Mike, aged 9, was enjoying the third art lesson devoted to modelling in clay. The rest of the class were into animals. Mike was absorbed in delicately raising a nipple on the breast of a nubile, kneeling maiden. 'A bookend', he explained. 'Can I do the other one at playtime?' Later, the bookends left to dry, he was duly congratulated. He was clearly gifted. There was almost a generation gap between his maidens and the distorted animals slowly sinking into their feet. 'Can I show me Dad?' he asked, and happily went home with them in a plastic bag. The next day he put them back on the shelf to dry. 'What did your Dad think, Mike?' He looked uncertain, as if unsure how to explain. 'Well, it's like this, the shape's OK but me Dad says it's all too smooth and round. Like this arm, see, it needs more planes on it to catch the light. Do you get it?' He didn't think that likely. 'Yes. What does your Dad do, Mike? That sounds like expert advice.' Mike nodded. 'He's a brickie. Really he's a stone mason but there's no call for them these days. I'm going to be a sculptor.'

Children frequently display an early interest in art, drawing and painting, modelling or making. Even during the earliest signs of this interest, sex-typing frequently takes place, so that boys are encouraged to draw cars and planes, spaceships and spacemen or to construct, whereas girls are encouraged to draw houses, ballerinas, horses and to dress dolls and play with models of domestic or culinary appliances. But it is rare for children who are not born into a home in which painting and drawing are practised, either by parents who are professional artists or who are keen amateurs, to be encouraged to develop specific skills of drawing, painting or sculpting. Turner, the son of a London barber, displayed early ability and was employed as a copyist in the home of Dr Monro the art collector, where he became friends with Girtin, before entering the Royal Academy School at 14. Sickert, whose father was a draughtsman and wood engraver, discouraged him from becoming an artist and, in fact, he began his career on the stage. Later, after entering the Slade, Whistler was his mentor. Picasso and Dali had artist fathers who recognized their early abilities and gave them both encouragement and expert tuition.

Thanks largely to the influence of Herbert Read (1943) and many distinguished artists, there has been, since the Second World War, an increased interest in children's art and in art education and schools have done a great deal to identify and develop talented pupils. Despite the influence of auctioneers, however, in driving up the prices of the works of the revered dead, the opportunities for young artists remain almost as precarious as they have ever been. In consequence, budding artists in the home are rarely encouraged to become water-colourists, oil painters or sculptors. Artistic abilities may well be directed towards engineering, architecture and crafts.

Scientists and Inventors

Whereas musicians and mathematicians may demonstrate their talents at a remarkably early age, scientists and inventors appear to have high general ability which may manifest itself early as an ability to learn languages and/or other academic subjects. Intellectual and scientific child prodigies often, but by no means always, learn to speak and read early, and show not only an ability to learn and retain what they have learned but also an eagerness to learn.

Many children display manual dexterity, have good spatial ability, enjoy making things and show curiosity about how things work or are made. Humphry Davy spent his youth in poverty in Truro, and was largely self-educated. He had wide interests – in fishing, on which he wrote a book, poetry and philosophy. He qualified as a chemist and at age 20 became superintendent of an institution for the study of the therapeutic properties of gases. Like J.B.S. Haldane, whose scientific career began when he became his father's assistant at the age of 8, he believed in experimenting upon himself, not always as safely and successfully as when he discovered nitrous oxide.

Edison's curious questioning caused his teacher to regard him as 'addled' and his mother removed him from school and taught him at home. He read quickly, had an excellent memory, built his own laboratory and sold papers to buy chemicals and equipment for it. His subsequent career as an inventor is part of modern folklore. The Wright brothers were in the same tradition of being largely self-taught and, like William Morris, Lord Nuffield, began their careers repairing bicycles. J.D. Watson, who shared the Nobel Prize with Crick and Wilkins for their work on the structure of DNA, was a child prodigy and radio 'quiz kid'. He entered Chicago University aged 15, graduating at 19.

Scientists and inventors, as we have already seen, display curiosity, persistence and single-mindedness, but the particular areas in which they specialize are often determined by chance. Early encouragement, exposure to a wide range of interests and opportunities to pursue their interests to the end are clearly important, but it is the depth of their thinking and their conceptual understanding which is significant. Parents who imagine that their child's interest in scientific television programmes is indicative of a scientific or inventive mind may well be misled. Being entertained is not the same as feeling compelled to examine and experiment, to find out for oneself.

It is vitally important that all children are encouraged to question and explore from their earliest days, and that they are introduced to scientific investigation in school from the outset. Here we are not advocating a discovery approach to education, but guided exploration appropriate to the pupils' levels of understanding. Later, science, engineering and technology can only be satisfactorily taught by highly qualified, enthusiastic teachers. The developments in craft, design and technology have opened up an important area of the curriculum and the development of courses with a vocational bias will undoubtedly tap talents and abilities in many more pupils. The abilities shown by pupils who have been exposed to projects in astronomy, the computer sciences and biochemistry, and those taking part in the Young Scientists of the Year and similar projects such as the Philips' Science competitions, demonstrate the talent which can exist once the staff and resources are made available.

Athletes

Prodigies in sport and athletics may well demonstrate their potential in infancy by their overall physical fitness, quick reactions, ball sense and agility. They may also display personality characteristics such as courage, perseverance and determination to succeed. But they will have to wait until they have developed physically before demonstrating where their specific talents lie. Inherited physique may have a direct influence upon the range of activities for which a child is fitted: there are no short, fat basketball champions or heavyweight boxers.

Again, early parental example and/or encouragement are important, especially in highly competitive sports such as swimming, ice-skating and tennis. Boris Becker began being coached by Breskvar when he was 6 years old. Economic and cultural factors also play a considerable part, as in the case of cricket in the West Indies, hockey in Pakistan, table tennis in China, rugby in Wales and soccer in England, for example, providing both role models and mentors. Traditions in schools play a considerable part in determining the range of sports and athletics pupils follow. It is axiomatic that if a school or county appoints a coach of international standing in a particular sport, there will be an upsurge of talent in that sport. The influence of Brendan Foster upon athletics in the North-East in particular and England in general is an outstanding example of that phenomenon. Whilst these factors have a general influence upon performance and the choice of activity, what characterizes young competitors is their determination to win and their devotion to practice in which the role of the coach or mentor is vital to their physical and psychological preparation.

The dedication displayed by, and achievements of, pupils and young athletes in the UK, particularly from West Indian and other immigrant communities, are readily applauded but not always given the early encouragement and support they deserve. It is interesting to note that, well before schools were thinking in terms of criterion reference testing, the Amateur Athletics Association (AAA) had introduced its award system which provided step-by-step goals by which pupils could monitor their own progress. Professionalism in sport and athletics, the worldwide media coverage of Olympic and other sports events have all contributed to a growth in the demand for the specialist training of athletes on the lines developed in the former Soviet Union and East Germany before unification. In this country, the setting up of residential schools for football and cricket prodigies had had a mixed response. The Football Association's national 'School of Excellence' at Lilleshall, Shropshire, has met with similar criticism to that made of all elitist ventures. Of far greater concern is the finding that 13- to 14-year-olds only get on average 10 minutes active physical education (PE) per week and that one in five school-leavers can't swim, according to the SW Council for Sport and Recreation's report. The Secondary Heads Association's survey of School Sport and Physical Education paints an even more depressing picture of the decline of PE and sport in our schools. Young athletes are having to become increasingly determined if they are to succeed.

Leaders

Leadership qualities are often revealed in play and games where organizing other children and initiating risk-taking are combined with verbal ability and a strong self-image. The stories of Clive of India's unruly boyhood typify these behaviours. Self-image may well contain a strong element of assertiveness, determination, single-mindedness, the need to achieve and be combined with a commonsense approach to problem solving. Colin Powell, who at 53 was the youngest ever Chairman of the US Joint Chiefs of Staff and chief military adviser to President Bush at the time of the Gulf War, is a first-generation American who was born in a Harlem tenement, during the Depression, to British parents from Jamaica, his father a shipping clerk, his mother a seamstress. He attributes his success to the values and goals of hard work and getting ahead, striving for perfection, seizing opportunities and learning from one's mistakes, which his parents inculcated. When due allowance is made for the fact that as a West Indian he may have had some advantage of status over indigenous black peers, his career has been one of remarkable achievement in leadership and administrative ability. Children who from an early age have had to take responsibility for themselves, say, through encouragement, as in the case of Richard Branson, or force of circumstances such as parental bereavement, may develop leadership qualities that enable them to get ahead in business, politics or the armed forces.

Social and Spiritual Qualities

Many children display caring and life-enhancing qualities. We recall R.J.O. Meyer, founder of Millfield, remarking on pupils of outstanding ability who had shown remarkable courage in the face of great familial problems and who had gone about their academic and school responsibilities in a way which made clear to him that he had more to learn from them in this respect than he could hope to teach them. Most heads have had similar humbling experiences. Some children, too, display remarkable empathy for others. Empathy has two major components, understanding and sympathy, and there is no doubt a strong cognitive factor which enables children to intuit the emotions and problems experienced by others, including adults. Cooperativeness and helpfulness are qualities which may be developed in the home, particularly in large families, but some children exhibit these social qualities and insight into the needs of others no matter what their circumstances. These qualities, too, like the others we have examined, are at the end of a continuum.

Eason (1990) has examined, with commendable common sense, the 'psychic' abilities of children who seem to be able to read their parents' minds, anticipate accidents, 'see' departed relatives, or have imaginary friends. Whatever the explanation for these phenomena, there is no doubt that some children have remarkable powers of observation and of interpreting non-verbal communication which adults, including professionals, frequently underestimate.

Much more significant are the daily examples of some children's courage in the face of disasters such as flood, fire, volcanic eruptions, famine, earthquakes and accidents. Even as we write, an award has been given to a 14-year-old boy who was babysitting when the house was struck by lightning and who, although himself burnt, rescued the baby by climbing through the roof. His brave example is typical of actions being carried out by children all over the world.

Many children, too, endure the pain and discomfort of multiple operations, chemotherapy or permanent disablement with incredible fortitude, often showing far more concern for the anxiety they are causing others or for those similarly afflicted than for themselves. At one end of the continuum are vulnerable children; at the other, are those invulnerable children who show fortitude, doggedness, confidence in their ability to survive, common sense in tackling difficulties and great concern for others. Radford (1990) cites the research of Werner (1984), who calls these children resilient. Vulnerable children we first encountered as those who succumbed to the schizophrenia suffered by their parents; the invulnerable children appeared immune and looked after their parents.

The example set and the standards and values of parents and teachers are important in recognizing, developing and encouraging these qualities of concern, responsibility, sympathy, understanding and courage in all children, vulnerable and invulnerable alike. It needs to be more than the hidden curriculum of schools and to be made explicit, not in the form of singing jingoistic school hymns but in the context of the ethical and philosophical education of pupils. Many schools, some under the most difficult circumstances, succeed in this and have developed the curricula and the ethos of excellence in all things because of their belief that education transforms children. This is comparatively easy in well-endowed, well-staffed and well-resourced schools where there is a unanimity of purpose between parents, children and staff. In many schools, however, these preconditions do not exist. It is interesting to note in this connection the relevance of the Philosophy for Children curriculum developed in the USA by Lipman (1980, 1988).

For some children, these qualities of concern for others have a spiritual component and they seek an outlet not only through good works but through wonder and worship or in a questioning concern for the ills and suffering of the world, which may be as much for its animals and plants as for its people. As one child protested to her teacher, 'You're always going on about the poor and the starving and the handicapped but they can speak up for themselves. What about the animals – they can't speak?' Another child, commenting on a speech by President Bush about ecological issues, thought he'd been 'waffling on a bit'. While some children show an early over-concern about spiritual matters, until they have developed intellectually it is our view that their wonder and curiosity be directed into a reverence for life, but preoccupation with death or the occult should be discouraged. We have not encountered any Bernadettes or Joan of Arcs, although we have known some who would have joined a Children's Crusade and have hastened to warn them of the disaster it was. We have been privileged to know children from whom we could learn qualities they seem to have been born and blessed with, like guts or the ability to cope with stress.

Parents and Prodigies

One of the difficulties in establishing what is hereditary and what is due to environmental influences in the development of prodigies is the unique one-to-one relationship between parents and child. This is not only direct, in that specific skills or achievements are taught, but also indirect, in that attitudes and values are an important part of the hidden curriculum of the home. There is a vast cultural difference between the home which encourages a child to grow up and be like his father and take his place down the mine and the one next door where, say, the parents are determined that the child will not go down the mine and, therefore, he must work, not play, strive to achieve and not be accepting.

The 'house next door' *may* produce a D.H. Lawrence or a musician, an athlete or an actor. Not only are there differences of child management and domestic regimen at play, there are different expectations, different incentives and different values. Moreover, it may well be that the match between these factors and the child may in one case ensure future success and happiness, in another success and unhappiness or in another failure and happiness. No matter how propitious the home circumstances, there are still so many other intrinsic and extrinsic factors that no-one can reasonably predict the outcome. D.H. Lawrence caught tuberculosis, a factor which also affected both his life and his art.

Even within the same home, parents not only treat their children differently but, even if they strive not to do so, their children experience their treatment differently. Radford (1990) has carried out a retrospective study of research by McCurdy (1957), Goertzel and Goertzel (1962) and Berry (1981, 1988) on the lives of distinguished people, and emphasizes the diversity of background and of early experience. The common factors included: early parental attention; early adult company; a rich fantasy life; early education; a troubled or disturbed childhood, such as financial or marital problems; parents with strong individual views; professional middle- or upper-class backgrounds; difficulties with schools and teachers; a religious family background, e.g. a Protestant or Jewish one which emphasizes hard work and achievement. However, Berry's sample of Nobel Prize winners found that the scientists, but not all his mathematicians and engineers, had made smooth progress through school and university.

Although research since Terman (1947) has emphasized the positive attributes of giftedness, it is important also to recall those gifted people who were born with disabilities – like Pope, who at 4½ feet tall and with a humpback spoke of 'that long disease, my life', or Samuel Johnson, who was deaf in his left ear and almost blind in his left eye – the many eminent people who have had epileptic episodes from Alexander the Great onwards, and those who, like Walter Scott and Toulouse-Lautrec, suffered either illness or a serious accident. Again, it is not surprising that, in the past, so much emphasis was placed on the role of adversity. Gorki was orphaned and, when he was 9, was turned out of his grandparents' home to make his own way in the world. At the age of 2, Samuel Butler was beaten daily by his clergyman father. Delius was one of 12 children who lived in fear of a sadistic father; his mother never showed the least interest in his musical abilities. Many successful people showed no signs of early promise. Wordsworth was a stubborn and intractable child, Coleridge was lazy and spoilt, Keats was wild and ungovernable and always fighting, and Darwin's father told him, 'You care for nothing but shooting, dogs, and rat-catching. You will be a disgrace to yourself and your family.' Perhaps, not surprisingly, the list of politicians who were late developers or did badly at school is considerable: Gladstone, Chamberlain, Baldwin, Roosevelt, Churchill, Bevin and Bevan.

By definition, prodigies are rare, the chances of them receiving the right stimuli and help from their parents are rare, and the chances of them subsequently receiving the right education and recognition are also rare, which is why genius is rare. That said, prodigies are ordinary children with some extraordinary abilities which, given appropriate nurture, enable them to achieve markedly higher levels of performance of those abilities than their peers.

For the results of many studies (e.g. Bloom, 1985; Freeman, 1986), we can characterize the intrinsic and extrinsic factors that *may* contribute to children becoming prodigies or young high achievers as follows:

- High general ability.
- Specific abilities such as in music, mathematics, athletics or art.
- The ability to learn quickly and to apply and retain what has been learned.
- Deep concentration amounting to absorption.
- Excellent memories.
- High levels of energy.
- Great interest and curiosity.
- A capacity for hard work and persistence.
- Pleasure in the mastery and performance of their abilities.
- A robust personality in the face of difficulties or setbacks.
- A sense of humour.
- A readiness to tackle problems and a delight in solving them.
- Parental encouragement and guidance in the development of application, work habits and discipline.
- Expert tuition.
- Insight into the conceptual aspects of their subject(s).

- An ability to go beyond the given information.
- Strong motivation to excel amounting to a sense of vocation.
- A feeling that it is only through these abilities that they can fully realize and express themselves.

Problems of Growing Up

The problem that prodigies may face is that of making the transition to the adult world in which they may not find continuing recognition and support – there's rarely more than one soloist in a concerto – and in which they may find personal relationships, in which they may be less skilled, in competition with their vocation. Realizing oneself through one's art may prove no substitute for procreation. It is this simple fact which makes so much of what is written about creativity appear trite and trivial. When one studies the lives of men and women of genius, it is common to note the strong sexual drives which influence their lives – a subject which escapes the attention of many researchers into creativity as if they believed genius existed in a perpetual Freudian latency period.

What this means for parents and educators is that, in the education of these children, attention must not only be given to the development of techniques, skills and knowledge, but it is of paramount importance that their social, emotional and physical development and health are continuously monitored. The very self-discipline, sense of vocation and dedication which these children show, may delude parents into believing that they are fulfilled by their art. When Jacqueline du Pré developed multiple sclerosis and could no longer play the cello, she was advised to develop new interests, to which her response was, 'God, the bloody fools! Don't they realize that's the only thing I can do, to play that damned instrument! *I know nothing else!*' No one could have foreseen that she would be so cruelly afflicted but they could have anticipated that she had earlier needed a richer and broader life than she had enjoyed, isolated with the cello she loved and the ritual of practice and lessons it demanded.

What prodigies need in order to be fulfilled by their art is to be fulfilled by life, by human relationships, companionship, friendships, affection, loving and being loved. They need, too, exposure to a culture broader than that limited to their own specific interest, especially when they are young and impressionable, curious and acquisitive. Three distinguished women, Kathleen Ferrier, Ella Fitzgerald and Margot Fonteyn, demonstrated by their lives – which were also marred by difficulties and tragedies – the sustaining strength that is gained by this broader, deeper exposure.

Between the doom-laden romantic view of genius as deviance and the neat statistical norms of longitudinal studies which promise that success-ful testees will become successful trustees of our cultural heritage, lies the truth of reality. The interaction of the uniqueness of individuals with the uniqueness of their environments is designed to create differences, not clones. Educating children entails educating them in excellence and giving them equal opportunities to realize their individual differences according to their multifarious abilities. These abilities are far more numerous and important than those identified by IQ tests alone, and education makes them more numerous and more important. Society needs them all, in abundance.

CHAPTER 8

Public and
Independent Provision

LEA Provision for Gifted Pupils

Many LEAs have a long tradition of making exceptional provision for gifted pupils in that they have helped them to take up scholarship places in grammar schools and choir schools, agreed to early transfers to secondary and tertiary education, and paid for pupils to attend national music or other specialist schools. Under the provisions of the 1944 Education Act, some LEAs, such as Hampshire, classified gifted children as in need of special education and placed them in independent schools. On the initiative of Bridges (1964), Brentwood College of Education provided enrichment courses for gifted pupils from Essex and the LEA's School Psychological Service was active in helping teachers to identify pupils, in organizing holiday schools for them and, exceptionally, in supporting their education in independent schools such as Millfield (Bridges, 1975).

The Schools Council project for Gifted Pupils in Primary Schools (Ogilvie, 1973) contributed to the growing interest in early identification and enrichment although, as with so many Schools Council projects, dissemination of the materials developed was never widely available in a generally accessible form. Together with the interest of HMI, it gave some endorsement to the legitimacy of the subject in the 1960s at a time when the sterile egalitarian/elitist debate was at its height. With the growing demand for the abolition of the 11 + and for comprehensive education – Anglesey opened Holyhead School in 1949 – and the pressure of successive Labour governments, this was important. At the time, the real educational issues, the quality of the education service and curriculum development, were obscured by political issues. The same old potion was being poured into new bottles.

Until that time, it was widely believed that grammar schools provided all that was necessary for gifted pupils and that the 11+ and IQ tests were infallible and intelligence largely inherited and immutable. Burt (1958), as we have already discussed, had argued from 1909 that not only was intelligence inherited but that it was highly problematic or largely a waste of time educating working-class pupils because of their poor genetic endowment. With the threatened abolition of the 11+ and the coming of comprehensive education, it is understandable that parents of gifted pupils felt their children were at risk. As we have seen, IQ tests are reasonable predictors of academic ability and grammar schools have never had any difficulty in selecting by 'scholarship' examinations pupils who have subsequently become in many instances outstandingly able professionals.

Burt's psychological research with its undercurrent of eugenicist views was largely unchallenged and even compensatory education in the USA, according to Coleman *et al.* (1966) and Jencks *et al.* (1972), appeared to have no effect on achievement. 'Compensatory education has been tried and it apparently has failed', claimed Jensen (1969). Although as early as 1945 Lorge had shown that schools in the USA did make a difference, it was not until 1979 that Rutter *et al.* established what many had always suspected, that 15 000 hours of education do make a difference in the UK as well. It is significant that those most demanding of the highest quality of education for their own children are so frequently those who dismiss it as of little value for others. Some of the most vociferous supporters of comprehensive education for the working classes sent their children to independent schools or moved into areas where they would be sure of a grammar school place.

Further confirmation of teachers' and parents' fears was given by the views prevailing at the time that disadvantaged families used a 'restricted code' rather than the 'elaborated code' of middle-class speech, thus further disadvantaging the disadvantaged. Although Bernstein (1970) could claim that his views were often misinterpreted, he too was of the opinion that education could not compensate for the inequalities of society. So much educational research and thinking at this time was characterized by the absence of intellectual rigour. Abstractions were treated as entities; hypotheses such as Bernstein's, which the history of the development of culture demonstrated to be insupportable, were used in arguments about educational policy. How could an agrarian society have been transformed by the industrial revolution without mass literacy and the innumerate mastering Euclid and Hall and Knight's

Algebra? How could we hope to raise educational standards without educating more children extensively? In this social climate, it is not surprising that the unplanned and unresearched demands by government to introduce comprehensive education was seen as a political panacea by the naive and as a threat to those who had a personal or vested interest in elitism. In many LEAs, the confrontation has still not produced a consensus and, unless you can pay for private education, 'where you live is what you get'.

The parents, teachers and educationists who spoke up about their concern for gifted children were drawing attention to the existence in schools of pupils who were being inadequately educated in large classes, who were not only failing to realize their potential but were also becoming bored, disruptive or disturbed. Schools could have a negative effect and, on the other side of the tracks it was being argued that disadvantaged children were being disadvantaged five hours a day, five days a week for 40 weeks of the year – by their schools. For parents of young gifted children, the nightmare was that they would fail their 11 + and have to attend a comprehensive school possibly on a split site or go to an unreorganized secondary school and they would never get to university. Support for their cause came largely from the USA, where the shock of the first Soviet Sputnik had thrown education into disarray and the search was on for new leaders, scientists and mathematicians. To this day, as we have seen, most of the literature in this country owes a great deal to US educationists and psychologists.

It was said at the time that the easiest way of identifying gifted children was to ask in the staffroom if anyone had bright kids in their class who were confounded nuisances. A more administratively potent method was to undertake surveys of under-achievers, but the common solution was to distribute checklists which served to alert teachers to the possibility that they should be looking out for these children and which gave some pointers as to what they should look for. Parents were becoming increasingly concerned, too, especially if they found that their children started school as enthusiastic and competent young readers and within a term had become disenchanted with reading and school, or were being held back in mathematics in lock-step with their peers doing pages of 'baby sums'. It was a time when many bizarre ideas abounded about surrounding children with books in the belief that they would learn to read, presumably by osmosis, and that it was wrong to teach children mathematics until they understood mathematics. Not surprisingly, the National Association of Parents of Gifted Children was founded in 1966.

Parents provided a valuable source of identification of gifted children in those authorities prepared to listen. As one educational psychologist found:

> When I told the boy's mother that she had nothing to worry about, he was highly intelligent, she said he couldn't be – his younger sister was much sharper and she'd not even started school. When I tested the girl she was right off the scale. No wonder the mother thought the boy was slow – and he's brilliant.

Frequently, finding the children and ascertaining how and in what ways they were gifted was easier than making provision for them. Once provisions were made for identifying these children and the word spread among teachers and parents, many more children presented as being gifted than would have been predicted by any measure of incidence. Even the psychometrician's Gaussian curve was thought by some, including Burt, to have a bulge at the upper percentiles!

But changes in education take a long time. In 1991, after three major education acts and five ministers of education in a dozen years, the retiring HM Senior Chief Inspector of Schools reported that a third of English primary and secondary schools had poor standards of education. It was reported that 9- to 11-year-olds were not being stretched, the assessment of children's learning was still ineffective in most primary schools, and in one in five of these they were still failing to teach reading adequately. Parents continue to have grounds for anxiety and, if they can afford to, turn to the independent sector or, if they cannot, make sure they live in neighbourhoods in which the schools are of a satisfactory standard. It is little consolation to parents of young children to learn from the above HMI report that GCSE and A level results are up. Parents are often acutely aware that it may not only be 'too late at 8' if their gifted children are ever to realize their true potential, but that, through boredom or not wishing to attract attention to themselves, they may well by then have fallen behind their less able peers. This is particularly true of musically gifted pupils at a time when the curriculum group for music, under Sir John Manduell, had to accept that music was a shortage subject and that LEAs may well have to cut spending on peripatetic instrumental teaching on which the country's pre-eminence in all aspects of musical education has been built.

While it is to be regretted that so much of the publicity for the needs of gifted children appears like special pleading for elitism, at the same time the protagonists have performed a valuable service in drawing attention to the shortcomings of the education service and by making valuable contributions to its improvement not only in middle-class but also in deprived areas.

Holiday Schools

Where, as in Essex for example, for a variety of historical reasons,
parents and the LEA have worked in harmony over three decades, much
has been achieved. Anyone who has been privileged, as we have been,
to assist at their holiday schools for gifted children will have seen what
this means in human and educational terms to the children. What so
many children find at these holiday schools is that they are not alone.
As one 10-year-old told us: 'Until I came here I thought I was odd. Now
I know I'm just like a lot of other kids . . .' He paused and added with a
grin, 'Odd!'

What characterizes holiday schools is the enthusiasm and curiosity of
the children. They relate to one another and to unfamiliar adults with
little if any difficulty because there is so much for them to do and they
enjoy being task-orientated. During the day they are busily involved
learning new skills or subjects or tackling problems set up in the
grounds, recording and filming their work as they go. Some are finding
for the first time that what they know about maths or geology, history
or biology is in demand; others are finding that, bright as they may be,
there are some things in which they are way below par, but no one is
criticizing – their own judgement is trusted (maybe not everyone is cut
out for glass-engraving or topology). Their energy and lively humour is
immediately apparent and during the day they seem to grow in stature
because of their involvement and commitment. Then, when they return
to their dormitories, they are suddenly small again, 8- to 12-year-olds,
with teddy-bears, story books or bits of wool comforters on their beds.

On one occasion, while they were getting ready for their evening
meal, a visiting speaker arrived to talk about nuclear power. During the
meal he was clearly worried that the talk he had prepared was unsuit-
able for these 'little children' and we tried unsuccessfully to reassure him.
He began hesitantly: 'As I expect some of you know, the smallest bit of
matter is the atom and . . .' and from one of the smallest children in the
room came the cry, 'What about the neutrino?' The speaker smiled with
relief. When it was all over he admitted he had rarely been questioned so
persistently and closely.

Essex has built up area working parties based in its primary and
secondary schools and its work for gifted pupils is co-ordinated by a
County Advisory Teacher for Gifted Education based at a Teachers'
Advisory Centre. The centre has issued some two dozen handouts for
teachers and schools dealing with a variety of aspects of the education of
the gifted including identification, the needs of different age-groups
from 4 to 16, curriculum enrichment and extension materials, problem-
solving activities, booklists and address lists of other organizations, and

LEA advisory teachers for gifted education. Over the years, the centre has become a virtual clearing house for advice and research in the subject and has a national and international reputation. Prior to her appointment to the University of Natal, where she is researching gifted-ness in the Zulu population of Natal, Belle Wallace was Essex Advisory Teacher for Gifted Education between 1978 and 1984. With her guidance, a third of Essex secondary schools and a ninth of its primary schools have implemented identification, enrichment and other procedures such as pastoral care for exceptionally able children, while others treat gifted pupils as having special educational needs.

One of the most interesting educational developments to come out of the work developed over the years in Essex is the whole school approach to meeting the needs of exceptionally able pupils.

The Whole School Approach

In brief, the whole school approach is concerned as much for children's abilities as it is for children with special needs. It starts with the identification of exceptionally able children and their various and different needs and, where necessary, counselling for them and their parents. Teachers are encouraged to look at how the children learn, the quality of their thinking, their individual differences, the results of objective testing of the children's abilities and careful observation using checklists. High intelligence, creativity, leadership qualities, abilities in the visual and performing arts, physical abilities and mechanical ingenuity and their interrelationship and overlap are considered. Distinction is made between the needs of children with a single specific talent, those with a wide range of skills and abilities, and those whose abilities appear to lie outside school subjects. School records, assessments and reports by educational psychologists or other agencies and particularly the children's performance on curriculum extension work are encouraged. Extension programmes are activities devised by subject specialists which are made available at lunch-times or at other times children are on the school premises and not attending lessons. In some cases, extension activities can be followed by pupils who have been excused other subjects. These activities should be intellectually challenging, go beyond the normal syllabus, should be self-directed and encourage independent thinking, leadership and communication skills and imagination. Ideally, the materials should be the result of inter-departmental consultation.

Provision should also be made for each child to receive regular individual counselling and pastoral advice to provide emotional and academic support. For the whole school approach to work effectively, it is suggested that a teacher should be designated as the responsible co-ordinator. The essence of the approach is to identify, support and extend each child identified. Clearly, it requires a whole school commitment and LEA support, and one welcomes the inclusion of the physically talented and those with abilities in the visual and performing arts in this thorough approach.

Other LEAs and Agencies

Most LEAs now have teachers or officers whose sole responsibility is gifted education or it is part of their responsibilities for, say, special educational needs or a specific subject such as mathematics. In the majority of LEAs, the School Psychological Service is a source of expertise and a point of referral for exceptional children, their identification, placement and problems. In addition to these psychologists, inspectors, advisers and advisory teachers, many universities, such as Exeter (or their schools or departments of education, as at Cardiff), and ex-polytechnics, such as Middlesex, have members of staff who run courses and/or undertake research in the subject. The Gifted Child Unit, Faculty of Science, Nene College, Northampton has been particularly active in producing specific advice on science for the National Association for Curriculum as well as on giftedness in general.

Identifying Able Pupils in the Secondary Classroom

An example of LEA and university involvement in school-based research funded by the Department of Education and Science (DES) is that undertaken by Denton and Postlethwaite (1985) in Oxfordshire, into the effectiveness of teachers' identification of pupils' subject-specific abilities in mathematics, physics, English and French. The research involved a close study of the top 10 per cent of a one year group of 13 to 14-year-old pupils studying this representative sample of important subjects in the secondary curriculum. Eleven schools, constituting an approximately proportional stratified sample of Oxfordshire schools, were involved.

This is a more important subject of investigation than might at first appear, because it highlights some of the central problems of school organization and some of the anxieties parents have had about what may go on in schools. If pupils are streamed on general ability, can it be assumed, as is often the case, that they will do relatively well, according to their stream, in all subjects of the curriculum? If we are looking for the top 10 per cent of 'able' students or the top 2 per cent of 'gifted' students, shouldn't we be looking at the top 10 or top 2 per cent in each subject? How can the gifted in a particular subject be identified if the work is not sufficiently challenging? What reliance can be placed on checklists for which no proof of validity exists? If validated checklists do not exist, how may they be constructed? How reliable are subject teachers' assessments of gifted pupils' abilities in their particular subject? The researchers reviewed the available research concerning these and other problems and identified the subject-specific tests they could use in mathematics. They describe the statistical devices they employed with the general aptitude (The Differential Aptitude Tests: Bennett 1974) and other tests used. Prediction equations were developed from the third-year test data available on two groups of pupils who had already gone on to take their O-level examinations, the results of which were known, in order to estimate, as accurately as possible from the pupils' scores on the individual test scales, the O-level scores that the pupils in the research sample could be expected to gain 2 years later.

The main results of this research were as follows:

1. The rate at which clues to pupils' ability occur in the classroom depends on the teaching style adopted; a large amount of class cooperation and discussion to develop a topic is most favourable, but this takes up a lot of time and recording observations is difficult.
2. In every class it was possible to make a full profile judgement of all pupils. In none of the classes were the teachers able to record clues to ability adequate for reliable identification.
3. Knowledge of pupils' abilities could be increased by (i) examining their school records and then engaging pupils in appropriate activities in the subject identified; (ii) if there were certain checklist items not filled in for a large proportion of pupils, the teacher could assess if the pupils were being adequately challenged on that aptitude. It was not possible in any school to identify pupils properly without engaging in (i) in a most deliberate way, but both ways were crucial.
4. Scrutiny of work-books gave a very limited range of useful clues.
5. An observer in the classroom can be of help to a busy teacher in plotting pupil profiles.
6. Pupils need to be given problems requiring the use of a wide range of knowledge or understanding.
7. When pupils have demonstrated their strengths in handling

problems such as those in (6) above, they should be given the opportunity to do classwork at that level and thereby be saved from the boredom and time-wasting of repetitive, routine work.

8. Using properly validated subject-based checklists, it is possible to identify pupils.
9. Proper identification required considerable application on the part of teachers.
10. Identification was concerned with the top 10 and 5 per cent relative to school norms, but this experience allowed the ready identification of high-calibre pupils relative to national norms.

From this careful and detailed research, it appears that if teachers are able to take the professional steps to know how pupils perform in their subjects in depth and breadth individually, then the identification of able pupils, based on classroom interaction, will be valid. Such identification, it is claimed, will be more predictively accurate than that based on a high IQ.

Among the other results of Denton and Postlethwaite's (1985) research, it is interesting to note that in the analysis of factors which might influence teacher judgement, it was found that: 'Perhaps the most powerful conclusion was that social class, neatness and sex did not appear to have an overwhelming influence on teachers' judgements in the individual schools.' Of the many variables examined statistically, no differences relating to type of school were found, and 'differences were more often difference from teacher to teacher than from one school type to another'. Having regard to the range of subjects involved, it was found that the number of pupils who have high ability in a large number of subjects was quite small. To allow for possible errors in teacher assessments when selecting pupils for, say, extension work in a particular subject, it was suggested that pupils about whom teachers are uncertain should be given the benefit of the doubt and included.

In English and maths, there was a high level of agreement between teacher-based assessments of pupils with high ability and subject-specific, test-based measures, but the teachers missed some high scoring pupils and included some low scorers. In French and physics, there was enough mismatch between the teacher- and test-based assessments to show errors of judgement by teachers. This gives cause for concern about assessment in all subjects where there is less opportunity to work with individual pupils than in English and maths. It was considered, however, that teachers could be helped by in-service training.

Because of errors in identifying or placing pupils of high ability in streams, it was urged that children should at least begin their secondary school careers in mixed-ability groups and that grouping on ability should only be made when enough information had been assembled to ensure that this was done in a subject-specific way, using a wide range of tests, teachers' opinions guided by appropriate subject-specific checklists and after teachers had received in-service training. In this respect, Postlethwaite and Denton refer to their earlier research, the Banbury Grouping Enquiry (1978).

Denton and Postlethwaite (1985) conclude their study by urging that if teachers wish to identify the abilities of pupils, they should:

- develop strategies that provide day-to-day clues to ability provided by challenging work rather than by tests;
- not underestimate the extra effort needed (i) in understanding the conceptual structure of the subject in detail, and (ii) in introducing challenges to the pupils that will give clues to abilities and relate these to the pupils' aptitude for the subject;
- use a teaching style that provides opportunities for work with individuals and small groups and for discussion with pupils;
- involve other teachers as second observers in the classroom;
- keep and use accurate checklists, subject-specific records which should be passed from year to year. They should be reviewed and modified as abilities develop.

The thoroughly professional nature of this school-based study is clearly apparent even from this brief summary of its conclusions. What is particularly relevant is not only that it contradicts a number of the myths that have grown up in and out of education, some of which we touched upon earlier in this chapter, but that it concludes with these words:

> We developed the notion that the group we were talking about might well be quite wide, however, but even more interesting is the point that if we scan through the major conclusions that are put forward from the study, for the main part we could offer these same conclusions for the education of *all children*.

NAGC Survey of Provisions

In 1989, the National Association for Gifted Children (NAGC), together with the National Association for Curriculum Enrichment, with a grant from the DES, carried out a survey of LEAs in England and Wales, which it published under the title 'Survey of Provision for Able and Talented Children' (1990a). The survey was in the form of a short questionnaire asking the LEAs to give information about the provisions they made for able and talented pupils and for those considered exceptionally able. Able and talented pupils were 'seen as around 10% of most able pupils either in general ability or in individual subjects'; exceptionally able were those who show 'very specific talents of an exceptional order and progress at an extraordinary rate in particular subjects or activities'. Of the 105 LEAs approached, 61 (60 per cent) replied. A number of LEAs said that other priorities prevented them from replying and two said it was against their policy to make provision. Of the respondents, 42 said they did make provision and 17 said that while they did not make provision for able and talented children, other agencies did so.

The survey provides a valuable overview of the diversity of opinions current in LEAs, ranging from the egalitarian to the enthusiastically elitist, as well as of the variety of provisions made for these pupils. However, such is the diversity even within this small sample (40 per cent of those approached), it would be unduly pessimistic to conclude that the position – of the gifted – in the LEAs who did not reply or who replied negatively was one of complete neglect. For instance, one of the strongest indicators of serious interest in the needs of these pupils is the designation of a 'contact officer' whose duties are exclusively or in part to provide for able and talented pupils. Altogether, 44 LEAs provided a contact name compared with the 42 who said they made provision for these pupils. Again, asked if they provided INSET courses for teachers or supported the attendance of teachers at courses on able pupils, 53 said that they did so. Similarly, although 20 LEAs did not have a contact officer for able pupils, 6 encouraged their schools to identify able children. In all, a total of 35 LEAs encouraged schools to systematically identify able pupils and 21 used a variety of methods including checklists, teachers' assessments and use of the psychological service. Exceptionally able pupils were identified by 20 LEAs.

Provision for the pupils was similarly varied. Enrichment was provided by 37 LEAs, 16 used support teachers in the classroom, 19 encouraged early entry to GCSE and 17 early entry to A levels. Setting or streaming was encouraged by 13 authorities. Here a distinction has to be made between what LEAs may encourage or discourage and what, in fact, schools may do. Acceleration was encouraged in 18 and early transfer in 13 LEAs. Withdrawal groups were encouraged by 17 authorities. A total of 26 LEAs said that some of their children attended courses at local institutions of further or higher education: 12 for maths, 5 for science, 2 for music and one for creative writing; one authority employed the part-time services of a Principal Lecturer as consultant for the very able. Those authorities which identified able pupils systematically were most likely to encourage structural means of provision for them.

Activities undertaken by these able and exceptional children outside school, such as music, drama, maths and science, were provided by 47 LEAs. Special provision for exceptional children including maths, chess and inventors clubs was made by 25 LEAs. Only three authorities supported a literary activity or sports. One may assume, perhaps, that some children talented in sports would be those taking part in the normal out-of-school games and sports activities and that others would be involved with other agencies, such as swimming and athletics clubs.

The pattern that emerged from the analysis of the replies was that:

> . . . the Authorities who had a designated person solely for the able were more likely to encourage the identification of ability and the use of structural means of provision than other Authorities, in particular those with no-one designated for able children. They were also more likely to support or provide INSET and activities outside school work and more likely than other Authorities to have contacts with Further or Higher Education Institutions.

The report of the survey includes examples of the excellent evidence provided by LEAs of their identification procedures, checklists, job descriptions for specialist advisory teachers and school co-ordinators for the gifted, structural and curricular measures including reference to the importance of 'compacting' – planning pupils' work to avoid repetition of what is already known – a statement of the needs of gifted pupils and an extract from an imaginative Draft Development Plan of a new borough authority, set up in April 1990, spelling out its policy aims for gifted pupils. The authors of the report conclude by setting their concerns in the context of the Education Reform Act and the advent of the National Curriculum:

> In the past dissatisfied parents of the most able might go to their children's school to protest that their children were not being 'stretched' and were bored or might even have presented confirmation of the child's high I.Q. in asking for more demanding work. Now they will be able to claim, with assurance, that their children can attain at Level x, y or z. The teaching profession will need to consider how to respond to such legiti-mate claims and to devise ways and means of providing for children well in advance of average peers of the same age. There is no suggestion in the National Curriculum that Key Stage targets should be age-locked and a flexible view of the ages at which able children can take examinations should prevail.

It is recognized, of course, that this, together with the need for teachers to provide for non-curricular subjects out of school time, has resource implications and needs the goodwill of teachers, active cooperation between parents and schools, and the 'encouragement by Central and Local Government of those people who put their policies into practice'.

Mensa and the Education Reform Act

Similar reliance is placed by Serebriakoff (1990) of Mensa and the Mensa Foundation for Gifted Children on the 1988 Education Reform Act, on the National Curriculum with its Key Stages and Standard Assessment Tests, on greater parental involvement in education, on opportunities for schools to opt out of local authority control and become grant (DES) maintained, and on the recognition of the special educational needs of gifted children. Writing from an overtly elitist standpoint in his attack upon what he calls 'the Procrustean egalitarian status quo', he forecasts that, under the weight of pressure from highly motivated parents: 'Schools with the poor records and reputations are likely to be avoided and fade away. The influential section of the British public is likely to become less passively tolerant of egalitarian, educational faddism in future. Those who still believe in it may stand and fight if they care to, but it is sure to be a lost cause.' Like Napoleon, whom he admires, Serebriakoff is 'thinking of the next battle' but one cannot but wonder if he has not, like Napoleon, underestimated the complexity of the issues and the strength of the opposition. Bernadotte was a wiser general and would provide a better model.

As the NAGC report makes clear, policy statements are one thing, but what is important is how they are put into operation and the quality of the services delivered. Understanding and goodwill are essential. Anything which is divisive and discriminatory can only result in resistance and confrontation. The simplistic notions of political thinking in black and white terms will not carry us far in an open society in which the sciences, the arts, the technocrats and bureaucrats, medicine and social services, industry and commerce, the physically disabled and the sensorily impaired, the universities both old and new, sports and the entertainments industry, and so many other legitimate interests are competing for their share of the cake and exerting their various influences upon education policies. The 1944 Education Act did not fulfil its hopes of educating children according to 'age, aptitude and ability', and selection and the 11 + were rejected not only by Labour councils but also by LEAs such as Conservative Leicestershire. The NAGC may complain that the Warnock Report and subsequent legislation have failed to make adequate provision for gifted children, but they might well ask what have they succeeded in doing for the mentally and physically handicapped they were supposed to help.

NAGC's Description of Good Practice

What needs to be addressed is, what should be done if all gifted children in our schools are to be identified, have all their needs met and all their abilities realized? Is it true that identification procedures, acceleration and enrichment, a specialist advisory teacher in every authority, setting, streaming or tracking, withdrawal groups and after-school activities, support for teachers and INSET, early GCSE and A levels and support for children at further and higher education institutions are all that is needed? The NAGC has provided a valuable service by making a systematic appraisal of educational provision for gifted children across the whole age range in a sample of state and independent schools which were considered to be examples of good practice. The report of the survey, *According to Their Needs* (NAGC, 1990b), funded by a grant from the Gulbenkian Foundation, examines and describes:

1. The concepts of giftedness used.
2. Views on the particular educational needs of gifted children.
3. How gifted children were identified.
4. Management and organization of provision for gifted children.
5. Curriculum and classroom practices.
6. Views of children, parents and teachers of practices experienced by them.

Altogether, 42 schools were nominated by LEAs, independent schools' organizations and by members of the NAGC, 28 of which were visited by the study team. A total of 12 schools were finally selected for intensive study, 6 of which were independent schools and 6 grant-maintained schools, covering the age range 3–19 years, in town and rural areas and providing different kinds of social mix. The report, without giving a qualitative assessment of particular schools, presents its findings in such a way that we are given a detailed picture of 'the varieties of practice current in various contexts'. Whether the reader agrees or not with the stance taken by the LEA schools and their dedicated staffs in the resources and methods devoted to gifted children, or with highly selective independent schools and their favourable staffing ratios, abundant material resources and high expectations of academic achievement, the report provides an opportunity for examination of how the needs of these pupils are already being met and what needs to be done before all schools are meeting the needs and developing the abilities of all children – whether gifted, able, average or having special educational needs.

If parents, school governors and local councillors are concerned that their LEA schools are at least as good as independent schools – and many of them, no doubt, would not think that was setting their sights high enough whether on social or curricular grounds – then the findings of this survey set against the background of what HMI found in their survey (see Chapter 1), make valuable reading. Clearly, what emerges is that the children in all the schools appeared happy and to be enjoying their education.

The biggest organizational differences between the state and private sector schools related to staffing ratios, in that the independent school classes were half the size of the LEA classes, and the majority of independent schools were selective in their entry – and this selectivity increased as age of admission increased. Not surprisingly, therefore, achievements were greater and over a wider range of curricular and extra-curricular subjects and activities in the independent schools. There was a social class difference, too: all the independent school pupils came from middle-class homes. However, what concerns us here are the measures identified in the report which were considered to contribute significantly to the education of gifted pupils. Here we are not concerned with the type of school, the fees or the examination syllabuses which, of course, were an ever-present factor in the education provided by the preparatory schools and which caused them, as the report acknowledges, to think more in terms of academic abilities and pupil groupings than in terms of giftedness *per se*.

In the sample of schools visited, many teachers recognized that gifted pupils had a need for personal fulfilment and development of their potential, but not only in terms of cognitive ability: they had needs to be children and to develop socially and emotionally, to be educated at least for some of the time with children of similar ability, to be stretched and challenged, but fully integrated with other children and helped to develop social responsibility, confidence and pride in achievement for its own sake.

Having an understanding, enthusiastic member of staff or head responsible for gifted pupils or a tutorial 'adult to adult' system for older pupils was considered a major determinant of successful identification, monitoring, records, parent and staff liaison, LEA support and ensuring the effectiveness of the school's provisions for the pupils. Regular discussion of the pupils' needs, their planned enrichment, placement in ability and withdrawal groups, etc., were noted in one school where the involvement of parents in the day-to-day life of the school and the stimulation of their children out of school were encouraged.

It was also considered important that staff members recognized that they could not provide for all of the needs of these pupils and that visiting teachers and lecturers should be utilized for music, art and games, as well as native language teachers. One comprehensive school had a 'resident' author and another planned to have a 'resident' artist.

The independent schools generally had more laboratories, computer facilities and libraries, and differences in resources tended to be greater between the primary and preparatory schools than between the comprehensive and public schools. However, the old established public schools had superior provision for sports, gymnastics, drama and music, whereas the comprehensives led in resources for home economics, technical, engineering and business studies, but they were deficient in microcomputers, language labs, textbooks, small equipment and had had to supplement resources through fund-raising.

Although the primary schools had mainly mixed-ability classes and generalist teachers, the most significant finding was that opportunities were there for work with gifted children through group work, individualized work in English and maths and free choice of work by the children. Setting for maths and English, streaming and other ability groupings were common after the age of 10. Specialist teaching was common in both the public and secondary schools and was introduced quite early in preparatory schools where there was no early grouping of gifted pupils but individual timetables and small-group tuition in musical instrument teaching, mathematics and unusual foreign languages with opportunities for early entry to GCSE O levels. The grant-maintained secondary schools used ability 'banding', set for mathematics on entry and for all subjects in years 4 and 5. The withdrawal groups in both the maintained primary and secondary schools provided learning opportunities for gifted pupils, which for them offset the disadvantage of mixed-ability classes.

The public schools offered an 'enormous number' of options and a lot of small-group work in the sixth form but regarded themselves as 'relatively mixed-ability' prior to the sixth form. The non-selective and selective secondary schools used withdrawal groups, had week-long expeditions, problem-solving and study-skill groups, and the withdrawal group curriculum 'extended well beyond the normal curriculum' in breadth and depth. This was only possible by staff giving up lunch and/or preparation and marking periods.

Opportunities for enrichment in the primary schools were provided largely in withdrawal groups and by some imaginative teaching and a broad approach to subject areas in which subjects such as English, nature study and art were combined. Gifted pupils' needs were met by the individualized work and free choice periods described above.

In the preparatory schools, the curriculum was largely dominated by the public school scholarship examinations, with French from 8 +, Latin from fourth year and Greek as an option in one school, but 'New' maths and Nuffield science were taught, and other schools had broadened the curriculum from the traditional examination subjects, introduced de Bono's CORT thinking materials, had a weekly chess lesson and an annual library project. Subject-based teaching was imaginative, lively and of a high academic standard.

In one highly selective preparatory school for the 3- to 13-year age group, the nursery department was Montessori-based and introduced French from the beginning which, like German, was taught by native speakers. Between the ages of 5 and 7 years, there was a transition to the more usual curriculum with art, crafts, drama, dance, music, PE and games, plus an extensive programme of visits at home and abroad directly linked to the curriculum and, in the upper school, integrated studies on significant themes. Here the whole curriculum was focused on enrichment and gifted pupils had individual tuition in special subjects and subject-specific withdrawal groups. Clubs were available at lunchtimes and after school, music was built into the curriculum and included Suzuki violin classes and orchestral work. The variety and richness of the curriculum of this school was partly ascribed to the close cooperation between dedicated parents and teachers and their single-mindedness in seeking ways of meeting the particular needs of individual children.

In all the preparatory schools, there was also a variety of extracurricular activities headed by sport and, in the boarding schools, inevitably, a very wide range of activities such as astronomy, electronics, jewellery-making, orienteering and caving which, of course, were not limited to gifted pupils.

Curriculum enrichment for the gifted in the two public schools studied was said to be founded on subject-based specialist teaching, in a largely didactic style prior to GCE O level, followed by a large range of sixth-form options – in excess of 40 in each case. In addition to the extracurricular activities mentioned above, many external speakers and performers were invited to the schools. In fact, while in no way disputing the quality and rich diversity of the educational opportunities available, it is misleading to describe them as 'curriculum enrichment for the gifted'. The resources were available for all pupils and part and parcel of the pursuit of the schools' pursuit of excellence. The quality and quantity of staffing, richly endowed resources, diversity of options and measures such as the assignment system and one-to-one tutorials, which allowed individualization of work, are precisely what parents expect leading public schools to provide for offspring being prepared for Oxbridge. In particular, the arts, music and drama flourished in both schools. With one very important proviso, the absence of engineering and technology from the curriculum, it is difficult to imagine a richer environment for pupils who respond to a boarding situation, whether or not they are gifted.

The curriculum of the comprehensive schools studied was broader, in that although fewer foreign languages were offered and the range of options at sixth-form was less, they had technical, engineering, business studies and home economics departments. It is in the science, technology and engineering curricula that the public schools appeared deficient and it is to be regretted that, with their outstanding resources, they still fail to see the opportunities they are missing both for their pupils and for society.

In the comprehensive schools, pupils could take up to four A level subjects, but the number of S level entries were fewer in the school which lost academically able pupils to the local grammar school. Despite this, both schools made specific provision for gifted pupils, there were many options available as part of the normal curriculum in the third and fourth years. One school had 100 entries annually to music exams, a music club, two choirs, a chamber music group, folk club and a string orchestra. There were two drama clubs and regular productions, and video work and theatre art could be taken at A level. Overseas and local visits and language and cultural exchanges were available. The business studies department had set up a school bank and building society and there was a community service programme to help pensioners, hospitals, playgroups and the handicapped. Both residential and non-residential outdoor pursuits were common, and over 100 clubs and societies operated at lunchtimes and weekends. Technical activities included a scheme for sixth-formers to teach managers computer skills, a TVEI project gave problem-solving work and there were visits to local electronics firms. A gifted pupil had been adopted and given a mentor by a local company.

Inevitably, the pace of lessons was slower in the larger classes of the comprehensive schools, but lessons provided opportunities for discussion, problem solving, role-play and follow-up research. Teachers with specialist skills and interests were brought in from other schools as contributors to lunch-time group and individual projects on a rich variety of academic topics. One school had satellite tracking facilities, while the other had an individual project on air navigation techniques. The Report (NAGC, 1990b) concluded its comments on the comprehensive schools by observing that, although compared with the public schools there was a 'somewhat less rigorous approach to formal academic subjects . . . the whole educational experience for gifted children offered breadth and depth, the normal and the unusual from among a wide range of components – and there was no doubt about the satisfaction of the beneficiaries'. This is high praise indeed when it is remembered that the richly endowed public schools were highly selective boarding schools and that one of the comprehensive schools lost high-ability children to the local grammar school.

Clearly, the 12 schools studied demonstrated to the researchers many aspects of what can be done to identify, enrich and facilitate the education of gifted pupils whether in a selective or non-selective situation, and the Report concludes by paying tribute to their excellent and often pioneering work and to the achievements and dedication of teachers, parents and pupils. What is not clear from the Report is how academically successful the pupils were or what the incidence of giftedness was in all its diversity in the various schools. The public schools, it appeared from the Report, were primarily concerned with academic achievement and neither they nor the parents thought in terms of giftedness save in the context of high academic ability. It is interesting, therefore, to extrapolate from this study those measures which appeared to impress the research team as contributing most to the successful education of gifted children.

What impressed the NAGC researchers most was undoubtedly the high academic quality of the education provided in breadth and depth in small classes by enthusiastic and highly qualified teachers supported by enthusiastic and committed parents and a wealth of resources, books and facilities with a rich variety of withdrawal and extracurricular activities. In this setting, they favoured banding, setting or some form of grouping to enable gifted pupils to be stretched, but failing this they welcomed the opportunities for individualized programmes and assignments.

Having someone responsible for the identification, guidance and monitoring of gifted pupils was desirable, especially in non-selective maintained schools, but such is the diversity of abilities and so varied are the needs of these pupils it was not possible even in the most richly endowed and generously staffed schools, to extend them without bringing in outside lecturers, performers, teachers and instructors on the one hand, and providing for carefully structured educational visits and community projects on the other. Flexibility in programming the education of gifted children, allowing for acceleration and enrichment, withdrawal and tutoring, where appropriate, were clearly advantageous.

There is nothing here which smacks of esoteric skills and recondite methodologies and not a mention of right hemisphere stimulation or crash courses in creativity. What is being predicated is good education that is appropriate to those with special educational needs because of their disabilities, to the generality of children and to those of high and exceptionally high general or specific abilities alike.

It is refreshing to find the Report largely free of political or ideological argument and see it demonstrating pragmatically what can be done in a variety of situations. Thus it goes a long way to lifting the argument for helping gifted pupils out of the contentious and confrontational and putting it into the context of the needs of all pupils and their parents.

Rightly, it dismisses the simplistic argument that it is enough to say that all children are gifted and therefore we should educate them all in the same way, and the naive view that gifted children will survive in any environment by virtue of their gifts. We should not throw out the concept of excellence and high achievement as the aim of education for all children with the bathwater of elitism and egalitarianism.

Paying for the Right to Education

Parents who can afford it have exercised their right to choose what they consider is in the best interests of their children. Some people may think they have chosen unwisely, casting their children out into often harsh boarding school environments which some parents would not tolerate; others may consider that they have conditioned their children to an exaggerated opinion of their worth in order to gain entry to the Establishment. Some will see dangers in hot-housing children. But in so far as we can see desirable and realizable qualities in some aspects of what these schools have achieved, we would be wise to wish to make them available to a wider range of children, either through such means as the Assisted Places Scheme or by translating their ideas and practices into state schools.

Just as parents have chosen excellent education for their children, so society may choose to make excellent education available for all children. Many parents who send their children to preparatory and public schools make considerable sacrifices to do so; all are paying for it. Society must be prepared to make similar sacrifices. We should also make sure that we have learned from the long experience of many of these schools, including their staffing ratios, curriculum planning, high academic standards and flexibility which accommodates individual differences of aptitude and ability. Certainly we will want to avoid any mistakes they have made or may still be making. In making these desiderata available for all our children, we will need to involve the professional skills and enthusiasm of teachers and administrators and the goodwill and commitment of parents and society generally.

At a time in our history when there is emerging a consensus for a much more highly educated population and a recognition that we cannot afford to neglect the education of our future leaders, scientists, engineers, musicians, craftsmen, artists, doctors and athletes – is there any skill or talent we do not need? – it is surely timely that we agree on the qualities of the education we need. We cannot tolerate or afford schools without adequately trained specialist subject teachers or sufficient textbooks or library books. We do not need administrative tinkering or ponderous legislation. The last thing we need is the imposition of unresearched, unplanned reorganizations such as we have had in the past. Of one thing, however, we must be sure from the outset: nothing will be achieved without a quantitative and qualitative improvement in the supply of teachers and the in-service education of existing teachers. There is no education without educators.

CHAPTER 9

Special Abilities – Special Measures

Schools are properly concerned with the education of children in those areas society deems important. Thus, for all children, we expect that their education will encompass English, foreign languages, mathematics, the sciences, history, geography, art and crafts. Gifted pupils with extraordinary abilities in these areas have been our main concern and what we have discussed applies in general to their education in these subjects. The National Curriculum is largely irrelevant to the needs and abilities of these pupils: they are operating at a level 2 or more years in advance of its Standard Assessment Tasks (SATs). What is important is that they are extended in depth across the curriculum, so far as is possible, and that they should be properly prepared for the appropriate GCSE examinations at O and A level without suffering the deleterious effects of hot-housing. In Japan, where the pressures of an out-moded curriculum and competition for places is excessive, about 500 pupils annually are reported by the media to commit suicide because they cannot keep up or have been unable to join in leisure activities with their peers.

However, there are abilities which, although falling within the curriculum, warrant special consideration. Musical, physical and artistic abilities may manifest themselves before formal education begins, whilst vocational and technical abilities have been neglected and are often subject to a watered-down curriculum. These abilities, moreover, appear to be those which have sometimes been considered as 'separate intelligences' by some psychologists and have been considered valuable gifts by the rest of us. We discuss below some of the salient aspects of the cultivation of these abilities.

Space does not permit a more extensive consideration of abilities such as those involved in dance, drama, film and the performing arts generally. Good schools have always fostered them, parents have traditionally made sacrifices to encourage them and society has always applauded them. Whether children aspire to be Margot Fonteyns, Vera Lynns or Jayne Mansfields, Nureyevs, Sinatras or Schofields, or to emulate their successors or the groups which weekly come and often mercifully go, what they need is a good general education, a proper education in the arts they wish to practise and in the life-skills and managements skills to survive in the business no business is like.

What characterizes the truly successful in any of these areas is their determination to succeed, their ability to handle success and their persistence in honing their skills. These are the components of professionalism which the public comes to admire and applaud. It is right, therefore, that the identification and education of these talented children and young people should be the responsibility of professionals and that their education should be as rich and rewarding as possible before they are eligible for entry to the centres of excellence, such as the Royal Ballet School, the Guildhall School of Music, Speech and Drama, and the newly opened School for the Performing Arts. Unfortunately, with the exception of a few cities such as Birmingham, the concentration of these schools and colleges is in London and there is a real need to establish a regional network of schools. Throughout their development and early careers, talented children and young people also need support, encouragement, advice and protection from exploitation. For many from working-class homes or rural areas, our proposals for mentors and patronage will apply. The quality of their education, wherever it may take place, should be subject to rigorous inspection by both professionals with appropriate backgrounds and by HMI.

Individualization Instead of Acceleration

While recognizing that some children benefit from skipping 1 or even 2 or more years, acceleration puts considerable strain upon some pupils. They may find making friends difficult and miss the friendship of their peers and they may be resented by their older but less able form-mates. Certainly, the opportunity for acceleration should be readily available for those pupils who may benefit from it, but their settlement and progress should be carefully monitored at all times. Schools with a real respect for the individual and for quality of personal relationships as well as for achievement have little difficulty in ensuring that pupils who have been accelerated are welcomed into their new forms and will prosper.

It is generally recognized that only those children who are considered sufficiently socially mature and psychologically robust should be accelerated. But this is not easy to determine in advance. Emotional maturity may lag behind social competence or acceleration may increase anxieties about failing or about standing out and being the conspicuous 'know all'. Moreover, some pupils may hide their feelings until harm has been done.

There are, however, alternatives which should be considered. Schools which set for subjects, for instance, can more readily create groups selected for ability and attainment irrespective of age, so that this becomes the school norm across the curriculum. Another alternative is greater individualization of instruction and work within the age-grouped forms. Diana's maths is 4 years ahead of her classmates and her maths teacher finds it hard to cope with work at her level. While remaining in her form with her friends, the majority of whom are as good as she is in other subjects, the head of maths has assumed responsibility for her maths teaching and for setting and marking her work. He acts in a tutorial role, discussing her work and guiding it.

With the National Curriculum as a guide, it should become increasingly possible to provide for more and more pupils to work at their individual levels in all subjects. This will be as appropriate for those pupils who failed to reach satisfactory levels in the previous year as it will be for the very able. Rather than stay down to repeat work, the less able can move up with their peers but continue to work at their own level. This has been the approach in primary schools and many comprehensive schools for decades. The National Curriculum should facilitate this and, it should be realized, many schools will find that most of their pupils are a year head of the SATs. No child should be held back in lockstep with the curriculum while all curricula are but a basis for revision and development.

Some pupils may also be given individual instruction by mentors. Wherever possible and appropriate, this should be done with the cooperation of the school. In such cases, rather than this adding to the hours spent on homework, it would be appropriate for the mentor to set and mark work to be done during school periods. Flexibility in arrangements such as this benefits both pupils and schools.

Special Abilities

Physical

In games and athletics, we see the importance of all the factors which contribute to giftedness. Without physical endowment appropriate to the activities, there is little that can be done to enable anyone to excel in them. Diet and exercise, practice and coaching can help everyone to improve, but if you are born with a pyknic physique you will never be a champion hurdler. Given appropriate physical characteristics, early identification and encouragement by parents and schools are important, and the greater the general ability the more effectively will the tiro benefit from instruction. The quality of coaching or training and the facilities for them will be crucial. Inspiring role models will play a large part in shaping development. Without determination, dedication, persistence, hard work and courage there can be no success. Extraneous factors, like being in the right place at the right time with the right abilities and preparedness, will play a part in determining success. Competing and cooperating with others of similar ability will be essential. Moral and ethical aspects cannot be overlooked and the intellectual and social development throughout the athlete's or sportsperson's brief career will be important for success during and after that active career.

Many schools provide excellent opportunities for children with abilities in games, gymnastics and swimming. Increasingly, however, the evidence suggests that a lack of properly maintained facilities and specialist staff shortages and the selling off of playing fields have prevented many schools, both primary and secondary, from providing the excellence of standards and the continuity which are essential for the physical education of the majority of children and for the identification and development of those with particular abilities and interests. Parental pressure and involvement can have a beneficial effect upon this situation and direct action by parents is often the quickest way of getting pools, fields and pitches up to standard and of convincing governors that a specialist staff is vital.

Physical activities are an example of the influence outstanding achievements by sportsmen and women can have by inspiring children to take up the activity seriously and by setting new standards to which they can aspire. The resurgence of interest in athletics in the North-East was largely the result of Brendan Foster's example and influence. Fortunately, general fitness apart, an early start is not desirable in these activities. Although many swimmers and skaters have begun to be coached early – some experts say too early – by enthusiastic parents, from 7 onwards children start to show their abilities in particular activities. This can only happen if they are exposed to them in the active sense, as opposed to passively enjoying the antics of wrestlers on TV or the tribal thrills and agonies of supporting their local soccer or rugby teams. How good children are at throwing a javelin or discus can only be known when they have the opportunity to do so.

This is also an area in which parents' encouragement and early coaching, whether in games like football, cricket and tennis or in running, swimming or skating, have always been important and again demonstrates the influence parents can have. But with increasing professionalism and the recognition of the dangers of injury or wrong instruction, parents may well start their children off and then wisely seek advice from the local athletics and other clubs about coaching and training. They should continue to ensure that balance is maintained between the activity and the child's educational and social development. If children have abilities they should not be subject to pressures to devote their lives to them to the exclusion of everything else: careers are short in sport and their education should prepare them both to enjoy and succeed in it and to have successful and rewarding lives when they no longer compete. It is also important that parents and coaches guard against the megalomania which destroys some outstanding athletes and educate them to handle the media and those who would exploit them.

Schools and clubs have been the traditional ways by which children with physical abilities have been encouraged and fostered. The setting up of special residential football schools has given valuable experience of the pros and cons for segregation in this specialist form of education. They may well improve opportunities for a small number of pupils to adopt professional careers, but this may prove to be offset by their divorce from the hurly-burly of playing in local clubs. Meanwhile, one can only applaud this determined approach to the pursuit of excellence and attempt to learn from it.

It is difficult to imagine building on this approach with schools specializing in, say, cricket, athletics or gymnastics. Certainly, any attempt to introduce the hot-housing once seen in the former nations of the Soviet Union and East Germany should be resisted. Ideally, as with all gifts, we would prefer to see them catered for in all schools and colleges, supplemented by the local clubs and organizations and the provision of playing-fields, swimming pools, rinks and sports stadia of international standard on a much more generous scale.

For many pupils who may not excel in the arts or sciences, physical activities give them opportunities to achieve. For many children in working-class areas and inner-city ghettos, success in games and athletics has often been the escape route to enjoyment and, sometimes, to success and acclaim. These pupils have been able to show not only their physical abilities but their dedication, sportsmanship and guts. They have often demonstrated, too, how ill-served they have been by their rudimentary education and how great are their intellectual abilities given the opportunity to develop them. It is a reflection on our educational system that they are often dependent upon hand-outs from sponsors and that they are not better provided for by schools and universities. The annual exodus to sports scholarships and professional coaching in the USA is a demonstration, if one were needed, of what should be provided here, with proper academic safeguards, were we seriously concerned with the identification and realization of our young people's potential.

Not all children enjoy physical activities, but the majority do and should be given a thorough education in them. For those with an interest and abilities in games and athletics, including pupils with special needs such as physical or sensory handicaps, this should be seen as an opportunity not only for self-realization through achievement but also as a way of tapping into and developing their other abilities and giving a sense of purpose, so often lacking, to their education. At the same time, we should not ignore the need of pupils gifted in other areas to take part in games and athletics. Good schools, whether independent or state, do this. All schools should.

Practical/Technical Abilities

> All these trust in their hands: and everyone is wise in his work.
> Without these cannot a city be inhabited . . .
> They shall not be sought for in publick counsel . . .
> and they shall not be found where parables are spoken.
> But they will maintain the state of the world,
> and all their desire is in the work of their craft.
>
> (Ecclesiasticus)

Michael Faraday had an ability of which little is made: from his father, a blacksmith, he had learned to make things and, throughout his career, he took pride in making his own apparatus and in designing and constructing his own experiments. It is a tradition of British science that improvisation has been put to such good use in the laboratories of our universities, such as that of Rutherford. But set against this is the other tradition that one shouldn't get one's hands dirty and that to make things is for the menials. In consequence, we have Establishment, industrial and commercial leaders, quite apart from senior ministers, who not only know nothing of science but who also denigrate practical skills. Moreover, many scientists, technologists and architects, for example, have qualified and practised without ever having had any practical experience or skills.

It is this gap which, in part, accounts for the gap in our infrastructure and our inability to put new ideas to practical uses. There has been a drift away from science and technology, as foreshadowed by the Dainton Report (1968), with the proportion of sixth-formers taking A levels in science and maths falling from 44 to 21 per cent between 1963 and 1990. Between 1985 and 1988, applications to study physical sciences at university fell by 8 per cent and by 20 per cent for engineering. But what is equally concerning is that, although we have one of the highest levels of achievement in science at 18, because of our system of three A levels as compared with nine or more subjects studied at the same age in, for example, Germany, France and Sweden, at 14 years of age English pupils come near the bottom of the science league table in the 23 countries studied by Postlethwaite and Wiley (1991) – below Hungary, Japan, Israel, Finland, Sweden, Canada, Korea, Norway, Italy and Australia. A similar picture emerges when the performance of 10-year-olds is compared in both science and mathematics. One of the reasons for this is our neglect of vocational/technical education. Another is the undifferentiated curriculum, without specific goals, for those with technical and practical abilities, which means that it is largely irrelevant to the careers of many of the pupils, over half of whom will leave school without any qualifications.

We recall a Building School set up after the Second World War to provide candidates for employment in the building industry. Pupils were selected at 11+ from those who had failed to enter grammar and techical schools. The first year was spent in practical work but from the second year, such subjects as maths, physics, chemistry, draughtsmanship and communication skills were introduced, building on the practical experience. Their examination results compared favourably with those obtained by the grammar school pupils and, instead of entering the industry as labourers and bricklayers with a few rudimentary skills, many went on to take City and Guilds and similar examinations. This was not what had been intended at all. Examinations were not for the 'hewers of wood and drawers of water' and the school, which had so successfully demonstrated what could be achieved by pupils of only average ability, was closed. Vocational education has been a dirty word in this country until recently and, even today, the approach is typified by the 'context-free' technology syllabus of the National Curriculum with its lack of specificity about materials and tolerances and the swing away from the practical subjects of GCSE in engineering, commercial and domestic subjects to the generalized craft, design and technology courses.

In Germany and Holland, with their long tradition of technical and vocational education, pupils learn to understand the nature of materials, their fitness for purpose, to take a pride in working in established procedures to predetermined tolerances and to gain satisfaction from making things. The exceptional schools in this country which have maintained similar criteria and have qualified staff and industrial, commercial or domestic machines, equipment and materials know how motivating subjects can be and have no difficulty in identifying pupils who show special abilities in them. We applaud the initiative of Hilary Steedman and Professors Halsey, Postlethwaite, Prais and Smithers in their Report, *Every*

Child in Britain (Halsey *et al.*, 1991), commissioned by Channel 4, which recommends that from age 14 there should be 'three inter-connecting pathways: the academic, the technical and the vocational' with opportunities to switch between them.

Their emphasis, too, on educating and grouping pupils according to ability, and for raising standards and the purposefulness of education for those who at present leave school with no meaningful qualifications and a sense of wasted years and failure, are particularly relevant to our concern for identifying and developing the abilities of those children who have practical abilities and who can grow into skilled craftsmen as dedicated to their crafts as musicians or sculptors to their arts. Tool-makers, instrument mechanics, model-makers, chefs, cabinet-makers, typographers and dress-makers 'maintain the state of the world'. We need them and those whose skills are ancillary to them, but whereas we have elevated the entrepreneur – who makes nothing but deals – to the peerage, we have had no adequate regard for the education of those on whose backs they live.

Children who are often quiet and undemonstrative but self-assured and have great patience and perseverance may show their talent by taking things to pieces and reassembling them and by their acute observation and interest in minutia. Although some may be slow to express themselves verbally, they may be quick and dextrous and seem to have an uncanny ability to conceptualize the three-dimensional properties of things. Their genius is rightly described as the infinite capacity for taking pains, but is informed by a sensitivity to materials and the inner nature of things. Some identify with the mechanical and electronic, some with the nature of living things, with plants or animals.

> Jennifer, aged 9, 'adopted' a wind-up gramophone, to which she devoted as much care as her sister gave her dolls, stripping it down and adjusting its mechanism before playing the small number of records she had and delighting at the changes of pitch as she changed their speed. Given for her tenth birthday an electronics kit suitable for teenagers, which, her parents thought, would occupy her for many months as they helped her work through the manual, she completed all its many experiments and constructions unaided before going to bed. But despite every encouragement from parents and teachers, she had no wish to pursue an academic career and became an antiquarian horologist.

> Gerald Wingrove, born in High Wycombe, his father and grandfather French polishers there, was always a whittler and loved making models. After an undistinguished school career, various jobs and National Service in the RAF, he was still making models and freelanced for Dinky Toys. Now, because, as he says, he enjoys making them, he makes model cars, valued by Sotheby's

at thousands of pounds, which have been described as the world's finest, 'exquisite in their perfection'. He has written two books on the subject.

Because the skills of manual dexterity and for making things appear to exist with and independent of other abilities, as in the case of savants, it appears to be a specific ability. Clearly, when combined with other abilities, it may have many applications and be of great value as in the case of surgeons. When the ability is absent, clumsiness and poor hand–eye co-ordination result in those butterfingers in whose hands things suddenly go wrong. When it is recognized that our economy lags behind so many countries, we will have every reason to identify and develop these gifted pupils whether or not they have outstanding academic abilities. Rigorous, hands-on technical and vocational education will free them from apathy and they will enter what Erik Erikson called 'active apprenticeship'.

Musical Abilities

> My mother was half-gypsy, half-Polish . . . It was probably through her gypsy blood that I inherited a passion for singing . . . I was only three but had the voice of an adult. I had been born with it.
> [From *Galina – A Russian Story*, by Galina Vishnevskaya (1986),
> the Russian diva, and wife of Rostropovich]

Children with musical abilities often declare themselves at an early age. As we have seen with both artists like Jacqueline du Pré and Treffert's 'extraordinary people', it is as if the music is their preferred form of expression, their language. Thelma Reiss, who died at Aldeburgh in 1991, had an early childhood almost as inauspicious as Vishnevskaya's. Born in Plymouth, her father was killed in the First World War and she was brought up by her mother. She suffered from malnutrition and had tuberculosis. Her mother was made aware of her remarkable gift when she played the piano by ear at 3 years of age, and when bought a small cello for £3 in a junk shop she taught herself to play. At the age of 7, after only 9 months' tuition, she played a concerto in public and at 13 won a scholarship at the Royal College of Music where she was supported by Plymouth patrons of music. For 5 years after college, she supported herself playing concerts and in cafes and clubs until, in 1930, her first recital at Wigmore Hall resulted in an immediate offer to play the Elgar Concerto under Sir Henry Wood. Thereafter, she played with leading conductors and orchestras all over Europe as 'the Great English Cellist' until ill-health cut short her career in 1955. Her story illustrates both the way in which early promise proclaims itself and the difficulties which may threaten its realization. It reminds us that the majority of musically gifted children are not born into the rarified milieu of affluent and influential families, but have to fight their way through all the difficulties and frustrations, all the lets and hindrances, with which the vast majority of us contend.

Imitation plays a big part in the early acquisition of music as it does in that of language. We can see this operating in the childhoods of great composers and musicians such as Bach, Beethoven, Brahms and Bartok. In folk music and jazz, many musicians, like Jimmy Yancey and Gil Evans, are self-taught and yet develop into innovators: Yancey with boogie, Evans as composer and orchestrator. There is, too, considerable evidence that musical abilities are both more widely distributed in the population and more universally admired than our education system reflects. The flourishing orchestras of the orphanages of Venice in the seventeenth and eighteenth centuries, for which Vivaldi wrote so many elaborate works, the Coloured Waifs' Home where Louis Armstrong learned to play trumpet so well he could challenge New Orleans' best, and those counties which have established youth orchestras demonstrate that there is no shortage of ability if tuition is available. That popular music can be sold in albums by the tens of millions, that churches use it for worship, armies to march to and the rest of the world to dance or work to, is testimony to its ubiquity and to the many levels at which it affects and is needed by the human psyche.

It is said that one can judge a good school or university by the quality and variety of its music. Without live music there can be no regard for the fundamental and finer qualities of life. It is also no accident that for all its post-war travail, Hungary should have such a high level of education – at age 14 the highest level of science education, with England ranking twelfth – when one recalls the contribution Kodaly made to developing its musical education. So it is lamentable that, whilst we enjoy islands of excellence, we have deserts of neglect in our education system. Again, it is often a case of 'Where You Live is What You Get', with many LEAs closing their instrumental teaching services and staff shortages. Yet, this need not be so. We know of schools, including residential schools for seriously behaviourally disordered children, where, because of the leadership of the head or of one or more devoted staff, the standard of music is high and it is an integral part of the concern for standards and regard for the realization of the pupils' self-actualization.

For parents who can afford tuition, finding a suitable teacher is not difficult, although, as we observed earlier, making the right match may take time and trial and error. Vishnevskaya's first teacher ruined her voice. Reiss was fortunate – her teacher was a Royal Marine cellist who brought her along soundly and rapidly; du Pré's first teacher wasn't a cellist. But the problem for many pupils is of combining education with their music. Church choirs, church organists and cathedral choir schools have helped many musicians. William Walton went from Oldham to be a chorister at Christ Church Cathedral, Oxford. The competition for places at schools such as Chetham's, Manchester, or the Menuhin School is great, and parents seeking advice about what is available should consult the Incorporated Society of Musicians (see Appendix).

Although evidence suggests that musical ability exists in all of us, some are particularly richly endowed. For instrumentalists, an early start at the age of 3 or 4 years is usually recommended, partly because of the ease with which its language and dexterities may be learned, very much as if the neural pathways had to be established, and partly because there is so much to learn. This is not to suggest that musical ability, on being discovered later, cannot be developed. Parental delight and pride in performance is vitally important in establishing the activity as being highly esteemed and, therefore, one in which perseverance is important. But parents and teachers also need to keep a balanced view of what lies ahead, protecting the young musician from too early exposure and exploitation and making sure that the musical and general education is broadly based. As they grow and develop, musicians may identify an affinity with a different instrument or become interested in composing, arranging or conducting or move from pop to chamber music. They may decide to take up chemistry or architecture. Keeping the options open and providing a wide education is essential. Poetry and the plastic arts, languages and the sciences should all feed the musical mind. Music does not exist in isolation but is an integral part of culture and society. The breadth of Menuhin's interests in music and its roots which he sought in Romania, gypsy music and India, the statesmanlike counsel he has exerted in musical politics internationally, and his contribution to musical education generally and at Trinity College of Music and his own school, is one example of the way in which a musician may play many roles. Malcolm Williamson, Master of the Queen's Music, a product of the Sydney Conservatorium and Sir Eugene Goossen's fostering, is a brilliant pianist, doctor of medicine and psychology and, *inter alia*, speaks six languages. If, as we believe, exceptional musical ability is a gift which some people are born with, it is a gift which has to be nurtured and developed but, above all else, to be enjoyed and to give enjoyment.

The Graphic Arts

Len was in his last year at comprehensive school and still having problems with spelling. To help him, the Head of the Remedial Department suggested he made some calligrams, drawing words to look like what they mean. With remarkable speed Len drew 'burst' like a row of exploding balloons, 'dump' as a heap of rubbish, and 'cliff', 'waterfall', 'canyon' and abstract words such as 'speed', 'darkness' and 'crazy' with telling wit. His draughtsmanship seemed effortless and the result of acute observation and imagination. Surprised, the head of department checked with colleagues only to find that none was aware of Len's ability. He made sure the Careers Department knew in time to get Len started in a drawing-office when he left school.

Len, with his sense of being a failure, had kept his ability secret. But an exceptional ability for drawing and painting in some autistic children and the fact that some children demonstrate early an ability to represent the three-dimensional world two-dimensionally or in models with remarkable skill, together with the fact that the art galleries of the world demonstrate to the majority of us how paltry are our abilities with brush or chisel, indicate the existence of exceptional spatial ability and, in painters, a sensitivity to colour. Artistic ability has been called 'the intelligent eye', but it is also necessary for that eye to be co-ordinated with an intelligent hand or hands. It is also essential that the ability, like all human propensities, has to be practised and educated. Education prevents the scientist from reinventing the turbine and the artist from rediscovering perspective. This education has to concern itself both with ways of seeing and with ways of representing. This, in turn, must be combined with an increasing understanding by the artist of his culture. Victor Pasmore saw the forces generated by the spiral in the tree he had painted and he wanted his pictures to break out of their frames. His subsequent exploration of abstract painting lasted many decades before he returned to more representational painting.

Since the Second World War art education has been seen as an integral part of the curriculum from nursery school through to comprehensive school. Increasingly in schools, there has been a concern for techniques and execution and a movement away from free expression which was thought to have some Freudian value in liberating children's ids, which they knew not that they had. In terms of art history, however, the post-war years have seen the increasing subordination of art to literature and philosophy. Appreciation of the pictures or constructions has depended upon one's ability to read and understand the catalogues describing them. Often, too, the shock of the new has tended to become the schlock for the few.

What began as *pour épater le bourgeois* became establishment art and, as Gombrich (1972) acknowledged, 'the shock has worn off and (that) almost anything experimental seems acceptable to the press and the public. If anybody needs a champion today it is the artist who shuns rebellious gestures'. When he quotes Quentin Bell (1964) protesting that 'there is no form of pictorial eccentricity which can provoke or even astonish the critics' and Rosenberg (1963) saying of the new Vanguard Audience, 'The tradition of the new has reduced all other traditions to triviality', he is underlining the problem confronting art education today. When we progress from Cizek's 'child art' and from preoccupation with the new, we see more clearly that art is not science and is another way by which man searches for and communicates meaning. It is within this concept that students must be helped to explore art and their responses to their universe. It is no easy task. Picasso saw that 'Every positive value has its price in negative terms . . . The genius of Einstein leads to Hiroshima.'

The development of the skills to communicate and the mastery of techniques must run ahead of that search for meaning so that it can be at the artist's service when he has found something to say. Finding something to say entails a knowledge of what has already been said, exposure to the cultures of past and present. The educator must keep the mind and the eyes of the student open, encourage initiative and experimentation, and foster excellence without blunting enthusiasm. Glib notions about creativity as self-expression need to be countered with a rigorous examination of the values of what is expressed and standards by which expression is achieved, by concern for levels of originality and the quality of execution. And because art is not science, the artist can no more afford to ignore the explorations of the scientist than the scientist can ignore the visions of the artist.

Parents can encourage and foster enthusiasm for art in its many forms and the early development of skills. They should seek out schools which have a concern for culture, foster the highest standards of execution and have an interest in each individual child. Although, so far, we have focused attention on art and artists, the underlying abilities which may first manifest themselves in drawing, painting or model-making may also develop in the direction of architecture, design, fashion or engineering. What is fundamentally important is a broad and sound education in the early years with progressive development of the specific abilities. If this is done, then when the time comes to decide whether the pupil should go to a university or a college of art, or study graphic design, fine arts or architecture, the decision can be made in the best interests of the pupil's development and abilities, and the choice will not be limited by inadequate A levels. As with all children's development, the quality of their teachers throughout their development is vital. In the words of William Blake, 'The eagle never lost so much time as when he submitted to learn from the crow.'

CHAPTER 10

What Needs to be Done

Education's Role

What we suggest is that we do something which has not been done by educational reformers before. Instead of dickering with the system for philosophical, psychological, sociological or political reasons, we argue for a pragmatic and holistic approach. If we examine where and how excellent education is delivered, we have a model on which to build. Instead of levelling downwards or selecting upwards, instead of imagining that the latest fads and fashions will prove to be a panacea, we should address ourselves coldly and boldly to recognizing that our universities, both old and new, our colleges and academies deliver excellence and quality in so far as they are staffed and resourced to do so. Our public schools and grammar schools, our successful comprehensives and sixth-form colleges deliver excellence because they are staffed, resourced and led to do so. As we have seen, the richness and diversity of their education is what characterizes them. Their unwritten curriculum is that pupils are different from one another and have different interests, sensibilities, motivations and personalities which must be provided for and developed. These are the models to which we should return again and again with not critical but with appraising eyes to determine how we should model our schools for all our pupils.

We start from the assumption that in a democracy all children are entitled to an education that will enable them to develop to the full all their diverse abilities. This places responsibility upon both the children's parents and upon society at all levels. Education is about the development of minds, faculties, propensities and abilities, about enabling children to become more able, skilled, intelligent, wise, sensitive, creative, interested, informed, knowledgeable, competent and able to access whatever they may need to realize their changing and unfolding capabilities. Education is about learning to learn by being taught the changing bodies of accumulated knowledge and skills by those who have themselves acquired and mastered that knowledge or those skills and the values and standards appropriate to them. Education in an open society is the facilitation of each individual's full development of those qualities of mind and sensibility, abilities and interests, gifts or propensities, personality and aspirations which he or she may possess. Education must have a purpose and that purpose must be clearly understood by those who pay for it. That purpose must not be politicized and limited to serving the industrialists or trade unions, the churches or the media, the bankers or brokers, the Establishment or a military junta, the political parties or one or some of them. It is essential, as the debates about the National Curriculum have demonstrated, that the taxpayers know. A government which bans the publication of a report it commissioned on the teaching of English loses all credibility.

In our society, with its limited democracy and elitist structure, where a largely docile public has limited access to information, education is a key to social advancement and greater democratization, the possession and control of which is hotly contested. That is why education has been politicized and reflects the sterile theories of political parties filtered through the ambitions of politicians whose preoccupations are with vote catching. But education makes us free and being free we can create and change our environment and our society. The central task of parents and local communities is to limit the politicization of education, free it from the control of politicians and civil servants and ensure that it is increasingly under the direct influence of the schools, universities and the professions concerned with education.

Education, the acquisition of knowledge and skill, equips us with the power amplifiers of thinking systems and the use of intellectual and physical tools. Not surprisingly, there are those who consider such power should be limited. They see history as the study of pre-selected information, not as methods of inquiry, science as a utility not as the falsification of previously held truths, and they want predictable outcomes for students, not the threat and excitement of unpredictable scholars who may go on to transform the areas they have studied and mastered. Education also needs, as we discussed earlier, a broader, deeper base than simply improving pupils' knowledge, understanding, enjoyment, imagination and morality. The nature of gifted pupils makes this abundantly clear.

The concept of education driven by market forces is so limiting and banal as not to warrant serious discussion. We have seen those unpredictable and uncontrolled market forces result in the Big Bang on the stock exchange, in widespread corruption, in bankruptcies, unemployment and homelessness. Politicians have been as incapable of estimating how many teachers would be needed and in what subjects they should be qualified as they have been in ensuring that enough cancer and heart specialists are trained. Again, so far as the latter are concerned, we are at the bottom of the developed countries' league table. So far as the training of teachers is concerned, three HMI reports (1991) have criticized the failure of courses to equip primary teachers to teach the science, history, arts and humanities curricula. And if, in a period of mass unemployment and falling exports, a government has been unable to ensure an adequate supply of the highly skilled workers industry requires, it is manifestly incapable of planning education. On the one hand, the DFE Statistics Department never knows how many sensorily and physically handicapped children it will have to provide for until after they have become of school-age and, on the other, the government has ignored the repeated advice of its top scientists about the needs for investment in research. It would be more sensible if education drove market forces and provided the skills and the know-how the economy needs.

That academically able pupils in middle-class areas are often adequately provided for should not blind us to the fact that pupils with technical, craft, art, musical, design and manual abilities are less well catered for and may often be discouraged from pursuing their interests. Nor should we ignore the fact that for 75 per cent of pupils, education has little to offer and is often in its final 3 or 4 years a bleak period with little relevance to their own lives or interest or to their future employment or further education. The possibility of a two-tier university system and of schools opting out underline the dangers of increasing this divide between haves and have-nots in our educational system. If this division was what the market or society needed, then there might be some slight justification for it. But the reverse is true. In Japan, Germany and Holland, for instance, the emphasis is on funding more research, of raising standards of scientific and technological education, and of improving the qualifications and status of those with scientific and craft skills alike.

We need look no further than the USA to see the effects of the policies currently being pursued. Politicized education has meant that US pupils have stood still in achievement levels since 1970, as revealed by the National Assessment of Educational Progress Report (1991) summarizing 20 years of national testing. Although during this period educational fashions have swung from the open classrooms of the 1970s to the back-to-basics of the 1980s, only 2.6 per cent of high-school seniors were capable of doing calculus or advanced problem solving. Over a third of twelfth-grade pupils were below basic attainment levels in maths. Only one in five eighth-graders had achieved competency in maths for her or his age level. As the then Education Secretary warned, 'What we did in 1970 is not nearly good enough in 1990.' Whereas Japan and Germany had developed curricula emphasizing advanced maths and science, the USA was, in the words of one educationist, 'acting as if America is still an agricultural society, and that all the mothers are home with their children'.

But the big tragedy of US education is what Kozol (1991) calls, in the title of his book, the *Savage Inequalities*. What causes these inequalities of bookless, broken-down, overcrowded classrooms in inner-city schools across the US is a lack of funding. And the reason for the lack of funding and the disparities between these schools and the schools in high-spending suburban areas is simply that citizens and politicians voted down tax increases which would have redressed the imbalance. There were no votes in taxing the rich to help the poor. Politicized education has resulted in disadvantaging the disadvantaged and the failure to deliver an education appropriate to the needs of society. Throughout the USA, the education service is in disarray and in some areas the desperate response has been to employ untrained graduates. It is a lesson we should learn and take to heart for it is already happening here.

Education is the transmission of our culture, which is much more than the shufflings in the marketplace – not that we should exclude them from consideration – and our aim must be to make as much of it available to each individual as possible to enable him or her to contribute to it. If we look at the outcomes of education at the highest level, we see at once that the purpose of the education of scientists, doctors, engineers or architects, for example, is that they should be equipped to contribute to their discipline or profession and go beyond its present limitations. Increasing knowledge and improving service are what being qualified in a profession is all about.

If that is the expected outcome of professional education, it should serve as a model for all education at all levels. We may recognize that not all doctors or engineers will make unique contributions, but we must educate all of them to enable them to do so if they have the ability and opportunity. Similarly, we recognize that not all pupils will be able to contribute something new to the trade or skill, profession or career which they follow, no matter how brilliant or assiduous they may be, but we should educate them to do so if they have the abilities and opportunities.

Parameters of the Problems of Educating Gifted Children

1. Gifted pupils are small in number and widely scattered.
2. Each gifted pupil is different and has different family and social backgrounds.
3. Giftedness may be focused in one discrete, specific area or be general.
4. Pupils have changing attitudes to their gifts and these changes may take place as a result of education, experience or maturation.
5. Gifted pupils are very demanding, often of themselves, invariably of others.
6. Gifted pupils need a rich and diverse education, no matter what their gifts, and exposure to a variety of stimulating and nourishing experiences.
7. Gifted pupils need the stimulation of similarly able pupils.
8. They also need the life experience of growing up with those more and less able than themselves.
9. Their social and emotional development should receive the same care and attention as the development of their talents or abilities.
10. Giftedness may not be accompanied by high general abilities, may be present in those with special educational needs and/or physical, sensory or mental disabilities.
11. Gifted children need educating, as do all children, in harmony between their levels of development, their internal drives and the instruction they are receiving.
12. Gifted children often escape into the success and enjoyment they get in the exercise of their gifts in order to avoid those activities in which they gain less satisfaction but which may well be of importance to their overall development and long-term success.
13. Over-zealous parents, mentors or peers may equally deny them opportunities to play games, socialize, relax or enjoy other studies or activities which may be vital to their overall growth and development intellectually, socially and emotionally.
14. Gifted pupils need educating by highly qualified teachers, mentors or instructors.
15. The education and development of gifted children should not be driven by the children themselves: nor can their compliance

in their parents' plans be assumed to be sufficient confirmation of their well-being or of their present or future happiness. Pleasing themselves and their parents may make them happy when they are young, but such a regime, especially when restricted largely to the development of a narrow talent, like playing the harp or ice-skating, may prove an inadequate preparation for the competing demands of adolescence or adult life.

16. Gifted pupils' parents may experience considerable stress and financial hardship if they are forever ferrying them to lessons and competitions and making exceptional arrangements for them. Siblings may feel neglected or jealous.

17. Gifted pupils' rapid progress may further deprive them of life-skills appropriate to their level of functioning in their particular talent. Thus, the gap between, say, a child's musical skill and her social maturity, may lead her to be exposed to crushing failure or international acclaim, at an age when she is too immature to cope with them.

18. Gifted pupils need to be prepared with a broad perspective of what may lie ahead of them in terms of careers and the various options which may be open to them.

19. Few gifted people achieve either the fame or the fortune to which they originally aspired, and pupils need forewarning of this and to be prepared for the possibility of having to settle for the satisfaction of more modest achievements. Chance plays its part with our genes and our schemes.

20. A sense of the mean, rare common sense, and balance are essential if gifted pupils are to be nurtured to develop their gifts in harmony with themselves, their families, their peers and society. Like everyone they are not immune to 'the slings and arrows of outrageous fortune' and realism and reality in their exposure to, rather than protection from, the harshness of life and mortality, may prepare them with the fortitude to survive. Gifts, they need to know, are not enough.

This may mean that for some pupils there will be a need to help them to access the curriculum. For gifted pupils, however, as for all pupils, the problem will be to provide a curriculum appropriate to their abilities.

Gifted pupils' abilities are quantitatively and qualitatively different from those of other pupils only in that they learn more quickly than their peers, retain what they have learned more efficiently and are able to apply and use what they have learned more quickly and significantly. If they are to be educated according to their abilities and not develop special needs, then these differences must be recognized. This entails great flexibility on the part of LEAs, schools and parents. The deficit model of needs is completely inappropriate. A limited concept of 'improving' education is equally irrelevant.

It will not be enough to state that because pupils are attaining the various Standard Assessment Tasks (SATs) at Level 3 in advance of their peers that they are, in fact, being educated appropriately. It will be necessary to ensure that they are progressing in harmony with their abilities, not in lockstep with their age-referenced criteria but in relation to curriculum-referenced criteria. Some 7-year-olds may need curricula appropriate to 14-year-olds. And, in this context, even qualified and experienced teachers cannot be expected to cope with pupils whose abilities span more than two stages.

If, then, we are to reinstate concern for the abilities as well as the needs of all pupils, it follows that we must look again at the abilities of pupils who have special needs and, instead of concentrating on what they cannot do, and giving them a lot of it, we should find out what they can do and use these abilities to help them succeed in meeting their needs. We must also look more closely and perceptively at the abilities of the generality of pupils and, using measures such as arousing their interests (see Chapter 6), explore activities in which they may achieve. There is enormous room here for recognizing that education is not limited to intellectual abilities and that society increasingly needs higher-order social skills, such as leadership, and qualities of personal responsibility, altruism, dedication and application, as well as physical, manual and spatial skills.

For the generality of children, we need smaller class sizes, greater resources and lively and well-trained teachers whose skills have been updated by frequent in-service training and who can advance pupils way beyond the levels of the present National Curriculum and transform that curriculum into something culturally deeper, broader and richer. This should also be appropriate to the diversity of abilities of the children and appropriate to the life-skills and the vocational and intellectual abilities they will need in work and in continuing education.

For gifted pupils, we need more than the outworn escape routes of enrichment and acceleration. What is needed is a whole child, whole education approach that is positively oriented to delivering excellence of instruction and the highest quality of education in the best discernible long-term interests of the individual pupil, with the minimum of disruption to normal family life so that neither parents nor siblings suffer.

What Can be Done

For a fortunate and privileged minority of gifted children, little needs to be done. These are children whose parents and teachers have identified their abilities and have provided for their development. They have gone to schools and colleges, to tutors or teachers best suited to foster their development, have had ample opportunities to live rich lives with stimulation and exposure to the diversity and richness of our culture, and have enjoyed living and working with similarly gifted peers and with those who share neither their abilities nor interests. In so far as some aspects of their development have been uneven, there may well be areas in which they need greater experience and, like all children, they need warm and supportive relationships during the transitional phases from infancy to childhood, from childhood to adolescence and from adolescence to adulthood. But for children born into affluent and cultured homes, the opportunities for the development of their talents are such that, together with their access to resources of expertise and advice and to careers, compared with the generality of children, they are well provided for. For them, whatever deficiencies they may have, society is an open society. That said, they may be exposed to the seductions of dilettantism or diverted from the full realization of their abilities into mandarinism or opt for a fuller, less demanding life. They thus enjoy the freedom to choose, although their choice may be their own or society's loss.

For the majority of gifted children, there is less likelihood of them being identified, greater difficulty in finding schools and teachers to develop their abilities, and often inordinate demands upon the time and resources of their parents and families. For them, the twin diets are enrichment and acceleration, holiday schools, and the scrabble for SATs, scholarships, assisted places and prizes. Instead of an open society in which the desiderata are there for the taking, as of right, they are, at best, in a lottery designed as an obstacle race from which they may be eliminated at any stage. Some may enter a system akin to Renzulli *et al.*'s (1981) Revolving Door Model, in which teachers assess their changing needs as they move from programme to programme. At worst, 'Where You Live Is What You Get' may mean they are never identified or, if identified, never given the opportunity to enter the race. Some will never be considered as gifted because they live in an area in which giftedness is thought of as high academic abilities only and outstanding talents in music, art, personal qualities, gymnastics, technological or social skills are ignored.

Surely there must be a better way of identifying and realizing precious human potential. Surely, too, the dangers of hot-housing and of isolation from ordinary social life can be avoided. Some pupils will be identified by their performance on SATs in the National Curriculum. But the prerequisites of educational development, outlined above, must first be met if more children with a greater variety of talents and gifts, skills, aptitudes and propensities are to be identified and developed. These can be simply stated:

- Additional more highly qualified teachers with specialist knowledge and skills.
- Smaller classes with greater expectations for pupils' achievements.
- Greater concern for the development of a much wider range of talents.
- Better school buildings, e.g. specialist facilities for science and drama, and class, subject and school libraries professionally staffed.
- A whole school approach committed to the identification and development of all pupils' abilities and the meeting of their needs.
- The total elimination of social inequalities which affect children's diet, rest, health, opportunities for play, etc., in their pre-school and school days.
- Positive discrimination in inner-city, depressed estate and poor rural areas to enable schools to meet the exceptional needs of pupils in these areas.
- All schools to provide evening and holiday extracurricular activities of a cultural nature in rich diversity.
- Maximum flexibility in the programming of individual pupils' education with termly reviews and updating.
- All LEAs to have specially trained advisers responsible for gifted pupils.

If these minimum requirements are met, the levels of all pupils' education will be considerably raised. In turn, this will assist the identification of gifted pupils and go some way to meeting the requirement for the realization of their abilities.

However, these provisions and resources will do little more than redress the inadequacies of the present compulsory school system. If the identification and education of gifted pupils is to proceed in harmony with them and their changing, developing abilities and needs, fundamental changes to the resourcing of their education is essential. Whilst in the vast majority of cases the intention is for the DFE or LEAs to be responsible for the pupils' education, there will always be LEAs and schools which cannot provide adequately for all their pupils' abilities and needs or which, for one reason or the other, lag behind in making adequate provision for, say, specific subjects or for in-service education. There is a need for the proper monitoring of educational standards and the quality of provision across the country on the one hand, and for the education of gifted pupils in all their diversity on the other. What we propose are radical developments which should change this.

Nursery Education

The most cost-effective first step, which has already been discussed, is the provision of nursery education for the children of all those parents who desire it. Ideally, this should be on a part-time basis; however, if necessary, it should be on a full-time basis. This, combined with parental involvement and support for those parents who for one reason or another find parenting difficult, would ensure that the abilities and development of all children were fostered in the early years and the effects of social inequalities minimized.

Depoliticization of Education

While political parties may have views about how much of the gross national product (GNP) should be spent upon education and about priorities for expenditure, educational philosophies, theories and practice should not be subject to vote-catching and the whim of transient ministers' instant expertise. They have had long enough to perfect their existing system and demonstrably it does not work. All parties should agree on a broad consensus for raising standards and for the development of educational provisions to allow children to realize their potential. Models of excellence in existing schools and systems here and abroad should be agreed upon and, where necessary, referenda taken. At both the national and local levels, education should be an all-party matter. This would ensure continuity, as opposed to the present system whereby one government legislates and the next delegislates and both act with scant regard to the effects they have upon the children and future generations. It would also ensure that, when policies are agreed upon or the recommendations of commissions are accepted, they are implemented.

An Enhanced Role for HMI

Given greater autonomy, strengthened in numbers and with members with recent research and university experience, HMI is the body which should advise on educational research and development and monitor quality control of delivery of education and teacher initial and in-service education. At both the national and local levels, it should work direct with policy makers. The role of the civil service and LEA officers should be concerned with administration. HMI is suggested for this role, which is essentially different from that of the *eminences grises* associated with payment by results, because its members are professionally qualified and experienced educationists who have the traditions and expertise to carry out the functions necessary. Their freedom from political influence and bureaucratic expediency should be protected.

Autonomy for Universities

Concern for excellence and freedom of research are essential character-istics of our universities. All-party responsibility for education should guarantee their autonomy and remove constraints, political and fiscal, upon their evolution in response to cultural change and upon their research. They should not be subject to the insidious influence of government-funded research.

Teachers as Professionals

Throughout, we have stressed the importance of the quality and exper-tise of teachers. They alone can realize the potential of our children. This will never be achieved while they are treated as second-class citi-zens: 'Pay peanuts, get monkeys'. To achieve the status appropriate to their importance, teachers must become professional, i.e. be responsible for (1) their own conditions of entry to the profession; (2) the control of numbers entering the profession and the subjects in which they are qualified and (3) determining their working conditions. They should also have the right to negotiate on their own behalf through their elected representatives and paid officers for the aforesaid and for their salaries.

Only in this way can we hope to see a continuous qualitative improve-ment in education and the end of the malaise of low morale, high wastage and progressive dilution. Without more and better teachers who have a professional commitment to delivering a professional service, there can be no real progress. Education cannot be led by market forces and inspired with the economic and philosophic naivities of the corner-shop mentality, nor should it be dominated by expensively educated manda-rins schooled in the cunctatory art of saying 'No' – very slowly – to all change which may rock their boats. Education must be led by profes-sional educators committed to educating for excellence and to the quality of the service they provide in the interests of their pupils and their pupils' futures.

Beyond the Ground-bed

With the emergence of considerably more gifted pupils in greater variety against a backgound of higher standards and a broader curriculum with wider extracurricular activities in our schools, there will still remain the problem of how to realize the potential of pupils who operate at two or more years in advance of their peers or who have abilities in areas not covered by the curriculum provided by their schools. As we have seen, none of the present methods of providing for them is entirely satisfactory in all cases and it must be said that, such are the differences between individual children and their circumstances, no provisions are ever likely to be ideally suited to all children. The best that can be hoped for is variety designed to meet the majority of needs and flexibility in adminis- tration. It is the quality of the measures that are taken which is important. The quality of instruction, the quality of cultural environment, the quality of social relationships and their diversity are what matter. Mediocrity, boredom, lack of arousal, the thwarting of curiosity, the stunting of originality, the denial of creativity and the tedium of trivia are the enemies of early promise. Schools, with their concern for the average, the norm and the mean, for the majority and for conformity, are ill-placed to cope with the exceptional, try as they might. They need extra support, expertise and resources – and above all, time, which means people – if they are to make any serious impact upon this problem at either end of the ability scale. How best can they be helped?

When we confronted the problem of 'dyslexic' and cerebral palsied pupils in schools we realized that it was useless to bay for the moon: we had to look for other available resources than specialist teachers and demonstrated how parents' natural skills could be developed to make dramatic improvements in their children's reading, speech and mobility/ dexterity abilities. This is not to deny the importance of the expertise of speech therapists, physiotherapists and other expert teachers, but to demonstrate how their skills and insights may be transmitted by parents given proper advice and support. With gifted pupils, however, although many parents have demonstrated how much can be achieved, this is only possible when they possess the knowledge and abilities in, say, maths, music or swimming, and have the time and opportunity to teach them. Even then, there may well be the possibility, as we have seen, that the children suffer the effects of hot-housing, or they reach the stage at which they need more expert coaching. Rarely are parents able to develop all their children's abilities and provide them with the variety of social and cultural experience appropriate to the children's development. Rarer still are the parents who can alone develop all their children's abilities and meet all their needs without considerable sacrifice themselves, without making inordinate demands upon other members of the family and without recourse to others for help and advice.

But what is clear in the education of gifted children born into privileged circumstances in which, from the outset, they are identified early and given every possible help and encouragement to develop their talents, is that they also enjoy the benefits of access in their open society to all the expert help and advice they wish. For the elite, society is open: advice is given, expertise is available, opportunities are created. Instead of trying to tinker with school timetables and organization, we should emulate this successful practice, improve upon any deficiencies it may have and make similar resources available as economically and efficiently as possible.

The three vital ingredients are funding, information and service delivery. When Beveridge (1943) drafted his celebrated Report, *Social Insurance and Allied Services*, which laid the foundations of our social services and 'welfare state', he recognized that there would always be areas and new needs which were not covered by blanket provision. In consequence, his subsequent Report, *Voluntary Action*, recommended that interested groups should make good these deficiencies. Charities are registered to provide for the relief of poverty, for religious purposes, for educational purposes and other purposes not covered by these. Another approach, in sports and the arts, has been patronage or sponsorship. Sponsorship is a recognized form of promoting the education of entrants to the armed forces and to industry and commerce by sandwich and other schemes.

Patronage

We propose that a nationwide scheme be developed to provide funds for the education of all exceptionally gifted children. Industry, financial and commercial interests, together with professional, trade union and other bodies, such as those from the media, would be encouraged to contribute to the fund. This broadly based resource would, by its very nature, ensure that giftedness was not limited to the narrow confines of high academic ability but would be concerned equally with sponsoring the education and training of leadership, technical and mechanical abilities, the arts – including the performing arts – physical and athletic abilities, and social qualities and would attract those who had a vested interest in the developing of new skills and abilities. Because of the broad base and the involvement of the bodies we iterate below, the dangers of hot-housing and over-specialization would be minimized. This would be an opportunity for the greater and more direct involvement of society in the growth and development of the sciences, arts and our culture. What is more, it could be done with the minimium of legislation, the minimum of bureaucratic delay and the maximum of efficiency.

The information would be provided by universities, colleges of art and music, professional bodies and by NAGC, Mensa and ECHA. Every LEA would have an Exceptional Pupils' Panel on which a nucleus of these bodies would be represented and on which the others would be called upon when needed. Their function would be to advise on and/or devise short-term and long-term educational and other programmes for gifted pupils which would ensure their overall education, having regard to their social, emotional and physical development, and the optimal development of their gifts or talents. They would, where necessary, provide mentors or instructors, coaches or tutors, and advise on curricula. Their remit would require that exploitation be prevented and that the health, happiness and well-being of the children and their moral welfare be of paramount importance at all times. Expert counselling of parents and professionals, such as teachers and therapists, involved with the children, would take into account the effects upon the family and ensure that financial and logistical problems did not result in undue stress.

The monitoring of each child's progress and development would be an integral part of the panel's responsibilities. Where appropriate, the provision of books and aids, such as scientific instruments, computers, musical instruments, specialist kits, etc., would be made by the panel, as would arrangements for travel in pursuit of pupils' studies, examinations, competitions or training. Wherever possible, retired researchers, tutors, lecturers and coaches would act as mentors to ensure the highest degrees of tuition with the minimum increase of workload on existing staff, but it would be essential that the direction of the programmes be in the hands of those directly involved in the particular subject areas or activities concerned. An essential function would be to ensure a match between mentors and pupils as they developed. As we have seen, the close identification of gifted pupils with their teachers is a sensitive and individual matter. Voices can be ruined, enthusiasm blunted and false starts made when there is a mismatch.

The overall aim of the panel to facilitate, in whatever ways it deemed best, the harmonious realization of gifted pupils' abilities and the meeting of their needs, would be in the form of specific recommendations. The implementation of these recommendations would be the responsibility of the appropriate LEA adviser and the panel would not have administrative responsibility. The recommendations of the panel would, however, be made available to the parents, school and all concerned and it would be important that its advisory and facilitatory function be seen to operate in the interests of the pupils independently and irrespective of LEA, DFE or other policies such as those of political parties or commercial interests. Referral to the panel would be through the LEA and its officers, including teaching staff, by parents or other interested parties. In making its recommendations, there would be the fullest involvement of the child and the child's parents or guardians and their concurrence would be vital before any implementation of recommendations was made. This last consideration would be essential if there were a conflict of wishes, say, between a child and parent. Where the recommendations were agreed by all parties but could not be implemented by the LEA through lack of funds or resources, the panel would be empowered to request funding from the sponsoring body.

Service delivery would normally be the responsibility of the LEA through its specialist inspectorial/advisory service. However, where pupils were attending independent schools and colleges or institutions outside the LEA's ambit, the panel might wish to appoint a mentor or tutor with responsibility for the overall supervision of the effective provision of its recommendations. What is important is that the panel's recommendations should be implemented in every way necessary to ensure the harmonious realization of the pupils' abilities.

The panel would continue to advise for as long as the pupils and their parents wished and, where necessary, they would advise on tertiary education and careers. A vital part of their role would be in facilitating the successful careers of those they had helped. One of the common problems of gifted young people is that of transition from the groves of academe to the cut and thrust of everday life, and everything should be done to help them find opportunities for the continued development and use of their abilities. This is not to argue for featherbedding, but to urge that where frustration and unnecessary hardship or wastage of ability can be avoided, this should be done in everyone's interest. What ideally should happen is that from the outset the advice and support given should prevent unnecessary division between education and the outside world, and that throughout there should be contact with the real world.

The funding, advisory and service delivery model we have outlined, based upon a sound educational system which is driven by a concern for quality and excellence for all pupils, is proposed as a major step towards making society more open, more truly democratic and improving the quality of life. It will require long-term planning and a complete rethinking of our priorities. It is this alone which will prepare today's children for the world of the twenty-first century. If we fail them, Britain will continue to decline in its standard of living, its social services and GNP will fall further behind and its status in the world of science, the arts, economics and politics will have dropped to that of a Third World state. Too much as been made of technological developments creating social change. We talk of the New Stone Age, Iron and Bronze Ages, Agrarian, Industrial and Information Revolutions, and forget that cultural progress has been made by people whose abilities alone have made change and progress possible. Realizing human potential is the only real revolution. Societies which continue to value and to develop their human resources continue to flourish; those which fail to do so fail. We cannot survive unless we change and adapt. The quality of life tomorrow is locked in the abilities of today's children. Education is the key which alone unlocks their gifts.

Bibliography

Arnold, K. and Denny, T. (1985). The lives of academic achievers: The career aspirations of male and female high school valedictorians. Paper presented to the *Annual Meeting of the American Educational Research Association*, Chicago, Illinois.

Ausubel, D. (1968). *Educational Psychology: A Cognitive View*. New York: Holt, Rinehart and Winston.

Baker, C. (1980). *Reading Through Play: The Easy Way to Teach Your Child*. London: Macdonald Educational.

Bennet, G.K., Seashore, H.G. and Wesman, A.G. (1974). *Fifth Manual of the Differential Aptitude Tests*. New York: Psychological Corporation.

Bernstein, B. (1970). A sociolinguistic approach to socialization. In Gumperz, J.J. and Hymes, D. (eds), *Directions in Sociolinguistics*. New York: Holt, Rinehart and Winston.

Berry, C. (1981). The Nobel scientists and the origins of scientific achievement. *British Journal of Sociology*, 32, 381–91.

Berry, C. (1988). Biographical databases as sources of information about exceptional achievements. *Proceedings of the London Conference of the British Psychological Society*, 19–20 December.

Blakemore, C. (1988). *The Mind Machine*. London: BBC Books.

Bloom, B.S. (ed.) (1985). *Developing Talent in Young People*. New York: Ballantine Books.

Boden, M. (1990). *The Creative Mind: Myths and Mechanisms*. London: Weidenfeld.

Bridges, S.A. (1964). *Gifted Children and the Brentwood Experiment*. London: Pitman.

Bridges, S.A. (1975). *Gifted Children and the Millfield Experiment*. London: Pitman.

164

Brown, P.T. (1987). Sexual development. In Gregory, R.L. (ed.), *The Oxford Companion to the Mind*. Oxford: Oxford University Press.

Bruch, C. (1973). The modification of procedures for identification of the disadvantaged gifted. *Gifted Child Quarterly*, 207–272.

Bruner, J.S. (1960). *The Process of Education*. Cambridge, Mass.: Harvard University Press.

Bruner, J.S. (1972). *The Relevance of Education*. Harmondsworth: Penguin.

Bruner, J.S. (1983). *Child's Talk: Learning to Use Language*. Oxford: Oxford University Press.

Burt, C. (1958). The inheritance of mental ability. In Tyler, L.E. (ed.), *Intelligence: Some Recurring Issues*. New York: Van Nostrand Reinhold.

Burt, C. (1964). Foreword: In Koestler, A., *The Act of Creation*. London: Hutchinson.

Chipman, S. (1988). Far too sexy a topic. *Educational Researcher* 17 (3).

Chomsky, N. (1968). *Language and Mind*. New York: Harcourt, Brace and World.

Coleman, J.S. *et al.* (1966). *Equality of Educational Opportunity*. Washington, DC: US Government Printing Office.

Denton, C. and Postlethwaite, K. (1985). *Able Children, Identifying Them in the Classroom*. Windsor: NFER-Nelson.

Department of Education and Science (1978). *Special Educational Needs* (The Warnock Report). London: HMSO.

Department of Education and Science (1977, 1989, 1990, 1991). HMI's Reports, Various. London: HMSO.

Eason, C. (1990). *The Psychic Power of Children*. London: Rider.

Easton, C. (1989). *Jacqueline du Pré – A Biography*. London: Coronet Books/ Hodder and Stoughton.

Eccles, J. (1987). Understanding motivation: Achievement beliefs, gender roles and changing educational environments. Paper presented to the *Annual Meeting of the American Psychological Association*, New York.

Edwards, T., Fitz, J. and Whitty, G. (1990). *The State and Private Education: An Evaluation of the Assisted Places Scheme*. Basingstoke: Falmer Press.

Eindhoven, J. and Vinacke, W.E. (1952). Creative processes in painting. *Journal of General Psychology*, 47, 139–64.

Ellis, H.H. (1904). *A Study of British Genius*. London: Hurst and Blackett.

Ellis, H.H. (1939). *My Life*. London: Heinemann.

Erickson, E.H. (1950). *Childhood and Society*. New York: Norton.

Erikson, E.H. (1971). *Identity: Youth and Crisis*. London: Faber and Faber.

Eysenck, H.J. (1971). *Race, Intelligence and Education*. London: Temple Smith.

Eysenck, H.J. (1973). *The Inequality of Man*. London: Temple Smith.

Feldman, D.H. (1986). *Nature's Gambit: Child Prodigies and the Development of Human Potential*. New York: Basic Books.

Feuerstein, R. (1979). *The Dynamic Assessment of Retarded Performers: The Learning Potential Assessment Device*. Baltimore: University Park Press.

Feuerstein, R. (1980). *Instrumental Enrichment*. Baltimore: University Park Press.

Fox, L. (1977). Sex differences: Implications for programs planning for the academically gifted. In Stanley, J., George, W. and Solano, C. (eds), *The Gifted and the Creative: A Fifty Year Perspective.* Baltimore: Johns Hopkins University Press.

Freeman, J. (1986). *The Psychology of Gifted Children.* Chichester: Wiley.

Freeman, J. (1991). *Gifted Children Growing Up.* London: Cassell Educational.

Galton, F. (1869). *Hereditary Genius: An Inquiry into its Laws and Consequences.* London: Macmillan (1982).

Gardner, H. (1983). *Frames of Mind: The Theory of Multiple Intelligences.* London: Paladin.

Getzels, J.W. and Jackson, P.W. (1962). *Creativity and Intelligence.* New York: John Wiley.

Goddard, H.H. (1914). *Feeble-mindedness: Its Causes and Consequences.* New York: Macmillan.

Goertzel, V. and Goertzel, M.G. (1962). *Cradles of Eminence.* Boston: Little, Brown and Co.

Gombrich, E.H. (1972). *The Story of Art,* 12th edn. Oxford: Phaidon Press.

Gordon, W.J.J. (1961). *Synectics: The Development of Creative Capacity.* New York: Harper and Brothers.

Gould, S.J. (1981). *The Mismeasurement of Man.* Harmondsworth: Penguin.

Guilford, J.A. (1967). *The Nature of Human Intelligence.* New York: McGraw-Hill.

Hadamard, J. (1949). *The Psychology of Invention in the Mathematical Field.* Princeton, N.J.: Princeton University Press.

Halsey, A.H., Postlethwaite, N., Prais, S.J., Smithers, A. and Steedman, H. (1991). *Every Child in Britain.* London: Channel 4 Television.

Hollingworth, L. (1942). *Children above 180 IQ Stanford Binet: Origin and Development.* Yonkers-on-Hudson, N.Y.: World Book.

Howe, M.J.A. (1989). Separate skills or general intelligence: The autonomy of human abilities. *British Journal of Educational Psychology, 59.*

Howe, M.J.A. (1990a). *The Origins of Exceptional Abilities.* Oxford: Blackwell.

Howe, M.J.A. (1990b). *Sense and Nonsense about Hothouse Children: A Practical Guide for Parents and Teachers.* Leicester: British Psychological Society.

Huizinga, J. (1970). *Homo Ludens.* London: Paladin.

Hyde, J. and Linn, M. (1986). *The Psychology of Gender: Advances through Meta-analysis.* Baltimore: Johns Hopkins University Press.

Janos, P.M. (1987). A fifty-year follow-up of Terman's youngest students and IQ-matched agemates. *Gifted Child Quarterly, 31,* 55–8.

Jencks, C. *et al.* (1972). *Inequality: A Reassessment of the Effect of Family and Schooling in America.* New York: Basic Books.

Jensen, A.R. (1969). How much can we boost IQ and scholastic achievement? *Harvard Educational Review, 39,* 1–123.

Kaye, K. (1982). *The Mental and Social Life of Babies: How Parents Create Persons.* London: University Paperbacks/Methuen.

Koestler, A. (1964). *The Act of Creation.* London: Hutchinson.

Kozol, J. (1991). *Savage Inequalities: Children in America's Schools.* New York: Crown Incorporated.

Krutetskii, V.A. (1976). *The Psychology of Mathematical Abilities in School Children*. Chicago: University of Chicago Press.

Laycock, S.R. (1957). *Gifted Children: A Handbook for the Classroom Teacher*. Toronto: Copp-Clark.

Le Bon, G. (1879). Recherches anatomiques et mathematiques sur les lois des variations du volume du cerveau et sur leurs relations avec l'intelligence. *Revue d'Anthropologie*, 2nd series, 2.

Lee, V. and Bryk, A. (1986). Effects of single sex secondary schools on student achievement and attitudes. *Journal of Educational Psychology*, 78.

Light, P., Sheldon, S., Woodhead, M. (eds). *Learning to Think*. London: Routledge.

Lipman, M. (1980). *Philosophy in the Classroom*. New Jersey: Temple University Press.

Lipman, M. (1988). *Philosophy Goes to School*. New Jersey: Temple University Press.

Lombroso, C. (1981). *The Man of Genius*. London: Walter Scott.

Lorge, I. (1945). Schooling makes a difference. In Tyler, L.E. (ed.), *Intelligence: Some Recurring Issues*. New York: Van Nostrand Reinhold.

Luria, A.R. (1972). *The Working Brain: An Introduction to Neuropsychology*. Harmondsworth: Penguin.

McCurdy, H.G. (1957). The childhood pattern of genius. *Journal of the Eleanor Mitchell Society*, 73, 448–62, cited.

Maccoby, E. and Jacklin, C. (1974). *The Psychology of Sex Differences*. Standford, Calif.: Standford University Press.

Makarenko, A.S. (1954). *A Book for Parents*. Moscow: Foreign Languages Publishing House.

Maslow, A.H. (1973). *Further Reaches of Human Nature*. Harmondsworth: Penguin.

Menuhin, Y. (1977). *Unfinished Journey*. London: Macdonald and James.

Merchant, C. (1980). *The Death of Nature: Women, Ecology and the Scientific Revolution*. London: Wildwood House.

Mill, J.S. (1873). *Autobiography*. Oxford: Oxford University Press (1924).

National Association for Gifted Children (1990a). *Survey of Provision for Able and Talented Children*. Northampton: NAGC.

National Association for Gifted Children (1990b). *According to Their Needs*. Northampton: NAGC.

Oden, M.H. (1968). The fulfilment of promise: 40-year follow-up of the Terman gifted group. *Genetic Psychology Monographs*, 77, 3–93.

Ogilvie, E. (1973). *Gifted Children in Primary Schools*. London: Macmillan.

Osborn, A.F. (1963). *Applied Imagination*. New York: Charles Scribner.

Parker, J.P. (1989). *Instructional Strategies for Teaching the Gifted*. Boston: Allyn and Bacon.

Parnes, S. *et al.* (1976). *Guide to Creative Action*. New York: Scribner.

Pask, G. (1975). *The Cybernectics of Human Learning and Performance*. London: Hutchinson Educational.

Piaget, J. (1951). *Play, Dreams and Imitation in Childhood*. New York: Norton.

Polya, G. (1971). *How To Solve It*. Princeton, N.J.: Princeton University Press.

Postlethwaite, T.N. and Wiley, D.E. (1991). *Science Achievement in Twenty-three Countries*. Oxford: Pergamon.

Radford, J. (1990). *Child Prodigies and Exceptional Early Achievers*. Hemel Hempstead: Harvester Wheatsheaf.

Rawls, J. (1972). *A Theory of Justice*. Oxford: Oxford University Press.

Read, H. (1943). *Education through Art*. London: Faber and Faber.

Reis, S.M. and Callahan, C.M. (1989). Gifted females: They've come a long way – or have they? *Journal for the Education of the Gifted*, XII (2).

Renzulli, J.S. (1977). *The Enrichment Triad Model: A Guide for Developing Defensible Programs for the Gifted and Talented*. Mansfield, Conn.: Creative Learning Press.

Renzulli, J.S., Reis, S.M. and Smith, L.H. (1981). *The Revolving Door Identification Model*. Mansfield, Conn.: Creative Learning Press.

Rogers, C. (1959). Towards a theory of creativity. In Anderson, H.H. (ed.), *Creativity and Its Cultivation*. New York: Harper and Row.

Rogoff, B. and Lave, J. (1984). *Everyday Cognition: Its Development in Social Context*. Cambridge, Mass.: Harvard University Press.

Rogoff, B. et al. (1984). Development viewed in its cultural context. In Light, P. et al. (eds), *Learning to Think*. London: Routledge.

Rose, S., Lewontin, R.C. and Kamin, L.J. (1984). *Not in Our Genes: Biology, Ideology and Human Nature*. Harmondsworth: Penguin.

Rutter, M., Maughan, B., Mortimore P. and Ouston, J. (1979). *Fifteen Thousand Hours: Secondary Schools and their Effects on Children*. London: Open Books.

Sadker, M. and Sadker, D. (1985). Sexism in the schoolroom of the '80s. *Psychology Today*, 19, (3).

Serebriakoff, V. (1989). *Check Your Child's IQ*. Cambridge: Mensa.

Serebriakoff, V. (1990). *Educating the Intelligent Child*. Cambridge: Mensa.

Shaughnessy, M.F. (1990). Cognitive structures of the gifted. *Gifted Education International*, 6, 149–51.

Silverman, L.K. (1989). It all began with Leta Hollingworth: The story of giftedness in women. *Journal for the Education of the Gifted*, XII (2).

Simon, B. (1971). *Intelligence, Psychology and Education*. London: Lawrence and Wishart.

Sisk, D.A. (1988). Children at risk: The identification of the gifted among the minority. *Gifted Education International*, 138–41.

Spearman, C. (1904). General intelligence objectively determined and measured. *American Journal of Psychology*, 15, 201–93.

Sternberg, R.J. (1979). The nature of mental abilities. *American Psychologist*, 34, 214–30.

Sternberg, R.J. and Davidson, J.E. (1985). Cognitive development in the gifted and talented. In Horowitz, F.D. and O'Brien, M. (eds), *The Gifted and Talented: Developmental Perspectives*. Washington, D.C.: American Psychological Association.

Taylor, I.A. (1959). The nature of the creative process. In Smith, P. (ed.), *Creativity: An Examination of the Creative Process*. New York: Hastings House.

Terman, L.M. (1916). *The Measurement of Intelligence.* Boston: Houghton Mifflin.

Terman, L.M. (1947). *Genetic Studies of Genius, Vol. 4: The Gifted Group Grows Up. 25 years' Follow-up of a Superior Group.* Stanford, Calif.: Stanford University Press.

Terman, L.M. and Oden, M.H. (1959). *Genetic Studies of Genius, Vol. 5: 35 Years' Follow-up of the Superior Child.* Stanford, Calif.: Stanford University Press.

Tizard, B. and Hughes, M. (1984). *Young Children Learning – Talking and Thinking at Home and at School.* London: Fontana.

Torrance, E.P. (1962). *Guiding Creative Talent.* Englewood Cliffs, N.J.: Prentice-Hall.

Treffert, D.A. (1990). *Extraordinary People.* London: Black Swan Books/ Transworld.

Vernon, P.E. (1971). *The Structure of Human Abilities.* London: Methuen.

Vishnevskaya, G. (1986). *Galina – A Russian Story.* London: Hodder and Stoughton.

Vygotsky, L.S. (1962). *Thought and Language.* Cambridge, Mass.: MIT Press/ John Wiley.

Vygotsky, L.S. (1978). *Mind in Society: The Development of Higher Psychological Processes* (edited by M. Cole *et al.*). Cambridge, Mass.: Harvard University Press.

Wallace, B. (1983). *Teaching the Very Able Child.* London: Ward Lock Educational.

Wallach, M.A. (1985). Creativity testing and giftedness. In Horowitz, F.D. and O'Brien, M. (eds), *The Gifted and Talented.* Washington, D.C.: American Psychological Association.

Wallach, M.A. and Kogan, N. (1965). *Modes of Thinking in Young Children.* New York: Holt, Rinehart and Winston.

Wallas, G. (1926). *The Art of Thought.* London: Jonathan Cape.

Weber, C.U., Foster, P.W. and Weikart, D.P. (1978). *An Economic Analysis of the Ypsilanti Perry Preschool Project.* Ypsilanti, Mich.: Monograph Series, High/Scope Educational Research Foundation.

Weikart, D.P., Bond, J.T. and McNeil, J.T. (1978). *The Ypsilanti Perry Preschool Project: Preschool Years and Longitudinal Results through Fourth Grade.* Ypsilanti, Mich.: High/Scope Educational Research Foundation.

Weikart, D.P., Epstein, A.S., Schweinhart, L. and Bond, J.T. (1978). *The Ypsilanti Preschool Curriculum Demonstration Project: Preschool Years and Longitudinal Results.* Ypsilanti, Mich.: High/Scope Educational Research Foundation.

Werner, E. (1984). Resilient children. *Young Children,* 4, 68–72.

Whitehead, A.N. (1929). *The Aims of Education.* London: Williams and Norgate (1950).

Whyte, L.L. (1962). *The Unconscious Before Freud.* New York: Anchor Books.

Wiener, H.S. (1988). *Talk With Your Child.* New York: Viking Penguin.

Wiener, N. (1953). The autobiography of an ex-prodigy. In Dennis W. and

M.W. (eds), *The Intellectually Gifted: An Overview*. New York: Grune and Stratton.

Young, M. (1958). *The Rise of the Meritocracy*. Harmondsworth: Penguin.

Young, P.W. and Tyre, C. (1983). *Dyslexia or Illiteracy? Realizing the Right to Read*. Milton Keynes: Open University Press.

Young, P.W. and Tyre, C. (1985). *Teach Your Child to Read*. London: Fontana/Collins.

Appendix: Addresses and Sources for Parents

Local Education Authorities

Details of educational services for children and young people can be obtained from Chief Education Officers or Directors of Education.

Enquiries concerning individual children are best made, initially, of head-teachers. Schools enlist the aid of support services, such as the School Psychological Service or the Advisory Service, for the assessment of children's special educational needs. The special needs of most children are met without recourse to the formal statementing procedures of the 1981 Education Act, although, in some instances, this may be necessary.

All LEAs are now required to issue details of the policies of their schools. Parents may request that their child attend any school of their choice, subject to there being vacancies. It is incumbent upon parents to seek the placement of their children in schools which best meet their children's needs and abilities.

Requests for grants for fees, books, uniforms and transport should be made to Chief Education Officers or Directors of Education. However, some schools, in particular older foundations, may have endowments, scholarships, awards or special funds to help pupils.

Applications for information concerning the government's Assisted Places Scheme, enabling selected pupils to attend independent schools, should be made to the Department for Education.

Independent Schools

National ISIS
Independent Schools Information Service
56 Buckingham Gate
London SW1E 6AG
(publishes guide to 1400 schools, *Choosing Your Independent School*, £4.95)

171

For parents overseas:
ISIS International
Independent Schools Information Service
56 Buckingham Gate, London SW1E 6AG

Most public libraries have current copies of the following and other year books:
 The Education Year Book, Longman
 The Independent Schools Year Book, A. and C. Black
 The Parents Guide to Independent Schools, SFIA Education Trust
 Which School? Gabbitas, Truman and Thring
 Whitaker's Almanack lists Headmasters' Conference Schools and their fees.

Teaching at Home

Education Otherwise
36 Kinross Road
Leamington Spa
Warwick

Home-Based Education Association
14 Basil Avenue
Armthorpe
Doncaster

National Extension College
Brooklands Avenue
Cambridge

Association of Tutors
27 Ladburn Crescent
Dunstable
Bedforshire

Organizations Concerned with Gifted Children, Curricula and Advice

National Association for Gifted Children
Park Campus
Broughton Green Road
Northampton NN2 7AL

European Council for High Ability
Bildung und Begabung e V,
Wissenschaftszentrum
PO Box 20 14 48
D 5300 Bonn 2
Germany

The Mensa Foundation for Gifted Children (Maintains list of mentors)
Mensa House
St John's Square
Wolverhampton WV2 4AH

National Association for Curriculum Enrichment
Faculty of Science
Nene College
Moulton Park
Northampton NN2 7AL

Foundation for Gifted Children
5 Makepeace Avenue
London N6 6EL

The Potential Trust
7 Bateman Street
Headington
Oxford

Advisory Centre for Education (ACE) Ltd
1B Aberdeen Studios
22–24 Highbury Grove
London N5 2EA (Contact The Education Law Advisers' Service at ACE)

Association of Preparatory Schools
138 Kensington Church Street
London W8 4BN
(Publish information on scholarships to independent schools)

The Incorporated Society of Musicians
10 Stratford Place
London W1N 9AE
(Music careers advice)

Department for Education
Sanctuary Buildings
Great Smith Street
Westminster
London SW1 3BT

Index